Breville Smart Oven Air Fryer Pro Cookbook

1000+ days of Easy-to-make and Tasty Recipes for Breville Smart Oven Air Fryer Pro | Bake, Broil, Air Fry and Slow Cook your Favorite Dishes with no Effort

Author: Chase Dunton

Contents

INTRODUCTION

The Breville Smart Oven Air Fryer Pro is the newest addition to the Breville line of small kitchen appliances. As the name suggests, the Air Fryer Pro is designed to air fry food with little or no oil. The Air Fryer Pro uses rapid hot air circulation to cook food evenly and efficiently. The Air Fryer Pro also has a dehydration function that can make dehydrated fruits and vegetables. In addition, the Air Fryer Pro has a bake function that can be used to bake cakes, cookies, and other desserts.

The Air Fryer Pro comes with a variety of accessories, including 13-inch Pizza Pan, Two Oven Racks; 9 x13 inch Broil Rack and Enamel Roasting Pan; Air fryer basket, baking pan, and dehydrator tray. The Air Fryer Pro is also compatible with various Breville accessories, such as the Smart Scoop ice cream maker and the Banana Bread Maker. The Breville Smart Oven Air Fryer Pro is a versatile kitchen appliance used to air fry, bake, or dehydrate foods. It is an ideal appliance for small kitchens or for those who want to save time and energy when cooking.

It is a top-of-the-line appliance that can make your kitchen life much easier. This oven uses super convection to reduce cooking time by up to 30%. That means you can get dinner on the table faster and less hassle-free. And because it has 13 cooking functions, you can pretty much cook anything you want in it. This oven can do it all if you wish to air fry, bake, roast, or broil. Plus, it has an included dehydrating function, so you can make healthy snacks like dried fruit or beef jerky. If you're looking for an oven that can do it all, the Breville Smart Oven Air Fryer is a perfect choice.

Benefits of Breville Smart Oven Air Fryer Pro

The Breville Smart Oven Air Fryer Pro is a versatile countertop oven that can do more than just fry food. It also has convection bake, roast, broil, and dehydrate settings. Here are 10 advantages of owning this appliance:

- ✓ The Air Fryer setting circulates hot air around food to cook it quickly and evenly, resulting in crispy food without all the oil.
- ✓ The Convection Bake setting bakes food faster and more evenly than a traditional oven.
- ✓ The Roast setting is ideal for cooking large cuts of meat or whole chickens. The Breville Smart Oven Air Fryer can accommodate a 12-pound turkey.
- ✓ The Broil setting browns and crisps food on the top without overcooking the bottom.
- ✓ The Dehydrate setting slowly removes moisture from food, making it perfect for preparing jerky or dried fruit snacks.
- ✓ Seven pre-programmed settings make it easy to cook a variety of foods with the touch of a button. These include chicken, steak, fish, shrimp, bacon, frozen fries, and pizza. Simply select the desired setting and the oven will automatically adjust the cooking time and temperature.
- ✓ The 60-minute timer can be set for longer cooking times and will automatically shut off when done. A sound alert will also notify you when the timer is up.

- ✓ An LCD display shows the cooking time and temperature so you can keep track of your food as it cooks.
- ✓ A non-stick interior simplifies cleanup and is also dishwasher safe for even easier cleaning.
- ✓ The Breville Smart Oven Air Fryer comes with an air fryer basket, baking pan, broil rack, dehydrating rack, and crumb tray – everything you need to get started making delicious fried foods at home!

Why Breville Smart Oven Air Fryer Pro is becoming famous

The Breville Smart Oven Air Fryer Pro is becoming increasingly popular for a number of reasons. First, it is an extremely versatile appliance, capable of air frying, baking, roasting, and dehydrating foods. Second, it features a number of advanced cooking functions, such as an automatic shut-off timer and precise temperature control. Third, the Breville Smart Oven Air Fryer is very affordable, making it a great option for those on a budget. Fourth, it is easy to use and cleanup is a breeze. Finally, the Breville Smart Oven Air Fryer comes with a one-year warranty, ensuring that buyers will be satisfied with their purchase. With so many incredible features, it's no wonder that the Breville Smart Oven Air Fryer is quickly becoming a household name.

Understanding the Structure of Breville Smart Oven Air Fryer Pro

The Breville Smart Oven Air Fryer Pro is the perfect kitchen appliance for those who love fried foods but want to avoid the extra calories. This oven uses higher temperatures and super convection to create crispy, golden air-fried foods. The Breville Smart Oven Air Fryer can dehydrate a wide range of foods. This is perfect for those who want to make their own jerky or dried fruits and vegetables.

It is a versatile appliance that can help you create healthy, delicious meals. Here's a closer look at its features and how they work together to give you the perfect cook every time. The Smart Oven Air Fryer has two fans that circulate hot air around food, giving it a crispy, golden finish. The top fan also helps to circulate moisture, so food doesn't dry out. The oven also has an advanced heat sensor that monitors the internal temperature of food, ensuring it cooks evenly. The Variable Crisp Control lets you choose how crispy you want your food to be, and the Auto Off function ensures your food doesn't overcook. The Breville Smart Oven Air Fryer is a versatile appliance that can air fry, dehydrate, and roast with ease. The secret to its success lies in its 2-speed convection fan. The super convection setting provides a greater volume of hot air, ensuring fast and even heat distribution. This is perfect for air frying, as it reduces the amount of time needed to cook food. The regular convection setting is ideal for dehydrating and roasting, as it circulates the hot air more slowly, allowing food to retain its moisture and flavor. With its wide range of cooking options, the Breville Smart Oven Air Fryer is a must-have for any kitchen.

How to Use Breville Smart Oven Air Fryer Pro A Quick Guide

The Breville Smart Oven Air Fryer Pro is a versatile appliance used for baking, roasting, and air frying. Here are 10 easy steps for using your new oven:

1. Preheat the oven by pressing the "Preheat" button. The default temperature is 400 degrees Fahrenheit, but you can change it by using the +/- buttons.
2. Place your food on the wire rack that comes with the oven. You'll also need to place the included air fryer basket in the oven if you're air frying.
3. Set the timer by pressing the "Timer" button. The default time is 30 minutes, but you can adjust it up or down as needed.

4. Once the timer is set, press the "Start" button to begin cooking.

5. When the timer goes off, the oven will automatically shut off. If you want to keep cooking, just press the "Start" button again.

6. To check on your food, use the included tongs to open the door and take a look inside. Be careful of hot steam when opening the door!

7. When your food is cooked to your liking, remove it from the oven and enjoy!

8. To clean the oven, wipe the interior with a damp cloth or sponge. The stainless steel exterior can be cleaned with any standard household cleaner.

9. To store your Breville Smart Oven Air Fryer Pro, just unplug it and put it back in its box. It's that simple!

10. And that's all there is to using your new Breville Smart Oven Air Fryer Pro! With a little practice, you'll be an expert in no time at all.

Understanding what you can cook in air fryer oven

The Breville Smart Oven Air Fryer Pro is a versatile appliance that can be used for frying, dehydrating, and even baking. It features several presets that make it easy to cook a variety of foods, from chicken wings to french fries. The air fryer function uses hot air to cook food, resulting in a crispy exterior and a succulent interior. The dehydrate function removes moisture from food, resulting in dried fruits and vegetables that are perfect for snacking. And the bake function can be used for everything from cakes to pizzas. Whether you're a beginner or a pro, the Breville Smart Oven Air Fryer Pro is an essential kitchen appliance.

Cleaning of Breville Smart Oven Air Fryer Pro

1. Remove the drawer and racks and wash them in warm, soapy water. Be sure to scrub the racks with a non-abrasive sponge to remove any stuck-on food.

2. Wipe down the inside of the oven with a damp cloth. You can use a mild oven cleaner if there is any stubborn grime. Always avoid using harsh chemicals on the interior of the oven.

3. Use a dry cloth to wipe down the door seal and glass door. Again, you can use a mild all-purpose cleaner if there is any hardened grime.

4. Clean the control panel with a damp cloth or an antibacterial wipe. Make sure you clean all the nooks and crannies to prevent dirt and grime from building up over time.

5. Use a brush attachment on your vacuum to clean the vents on the back of the oven. These vents need to be clear in order for the oven to function properly.

6. Once everything is spotless, reassemble the drawer and racks and replace them in the oven. Then, give the outside of the oven a quick wipe down with a microfiber cloth.

7. And that's it! You've now cleaned your Breville Smart Oven Air Fryer Pro from top to bottom!

Maintenance of Breville Smart Oven Air Fryer Pro

Congratulations if you've recently invested in the Breville Smart Oven Air Fryer Pro! This amazing appliance can do everything from baking to air frying to dehydrating. To keep it running like new, here are five tips for maintenance:

1. Always use fresh, dry ingredients. Moisture can cause sticking and clogging, so make sure your food is thoroughly dry before cooking.

2. Keep the interior clean. Wipe down the inside of the oven after each use, and give it a more thorough cleaning every few weeks.

3. Don't overcrowd the basket. When air frying, make sure there's plenty of space around each piece of food so that hot air can circulate properly.

4. Don't forget the filter. The air fryer basket has a removable filter that should be cleaned regularly. Rinse it in warm water

and let it air dry completely before putting it back in place.

5. Store it properly. When not in use, keep the oven stored in a cool, dry place with the power cord hanging freely so that it doesn't become tangled or damaged.

These simple tips will help ensure that your Breville Smart Oven Air Fryer Pro provides years of trouble-free service. Enjoy!

FAQs

✓ What is the Breville Smart Oven Air Fryer Pro?

The Breville Smart Oven Air Fryer Pro is an oven that uses hot air to fry food. It has a capacity of 2.5 quarts and can cook up to 4 servings at a time. Additionally, it has 8 pre-set functions and an LCD display for easy operation.

✓ How does it work?

The Breville Smart Oven Air Fryer Pro works by circulating hot air around food, which cooks it quickly and evenly. Additionally, the air fryer feature allows you to cook food with little to no oil, making it a healthier option than traditional frying methods.

✓ What are the benefits of using an air fryer?

Air fryers have several benefits, including being healthier than traditional frying methods, being more energy efficient, and being able to cook food quickly and evenly. Additionally, they can be used to cook a variety of foods, including chicken, fish, vegetables, and even desserts.

✓ How do I use the Breville Smart Oven Air Fryer Pro?

To use the Breville Smart Oven Air Fryer Pro, simply add your food to the baking pan or basket, select your desired cooking time and temperature, and then press the start button. The oven will do the rest, cooking your food evenly and quickly.

✓ What are some tips for using an air fryer?

Some helpful tips for using an air fryer include adding oil or cooking spray to help ensure food doesn't stick to the pan or basket, preheating the oven before adding food, and shaking or flipping food halfway through cooking to help ensure even cooking. Additionally, read the included manual before use for detailed instructions on how to use your particular air fryer model.

✓ Can I put foil in an air fryer?

Yes, you can put foil in an air fryer. However, be sure to avoid touching the heating element with foil as this could cause a fire. Additionally, make sure there is enough space between pieces of foil so that hot air can circulate properly. Finally, always remove any excess grease from foil before placing it in the air fryer, as this could also cause a fire.

✓ Can I put metal in an air fryer?

In general, you should avoid putting metal in an air fryer as this could cause a fire. However, some models may have special racks or pans that are designed for use with metal utensils or cookware. Always check your manual for specific instructions on what type of cookware is safe to use with your particular model of air fryer.

✓ Is an air fryer safe?

Air fryers are generally safe to use when operated according to manufacturer's instructions; however, there is always a risk of fire when using any type of appliance that produces heat. Be sure to read all manuals and warnings before use carefully, and never leave your air fryer unattended while in use. If you notice any damage or signs of wear on your air fryer, discontinue use immediately and contact the manufacturer for further instructions.

✓ **Can I leave my air fryer on overnight?**

No, you should never leave your air fryer on overnight or unattended while in use as this could result in a fire. If you need to leave your home while your air fryer is in use, turn it off first.

✓ **Where can I find more information about using my Breville Smart Oven Air Fryer?**

Please consult the included manual or contact customer service for more information about using your Breville Smart Oven Air Fryer. Additional troubleshooting information may also be available online at www .brevilleusa.com

BREAKFAST RECIPES

OATS & NUTS GRANOLA

Prep Time: 15 mins.| Cook Time: 15 mins.| Serves: 8

- ✓ 1/3 C. olive oil
- ✓ ¼ C. maple syrup
- ✓ 2 tbsp. honey
- ✓ ½ tsp. vanilla extract
- ✓ 2 C. rolled oats
- ✓ ½ C. wheat germ, toasted
- ✓ ¼ C. dried cherries
- ✓ ¼ C. dried blueberries
- ✓ 2 tbsp. dried cranberries
- ✓ 2 tbsp. sunflower seeds
- ✓ 2 tbsp. pumpkin seeds, shelled
- ✓ 1 tbsp. flaxseeds
- ✓ 2 tbsp. pecans, chopped
- ✓ 2 tbsp. hazelnuts, chopped
- ✓ 2 tbsp. almonds, chopped
- ✓ 2 tbsp. walnuts, chopped
- ✓ ½ tsp. ground cinnamon
- ✓ 1/8 tsp. ground ginger

1. In a small-sized bowl, add oil and maple syrup and mix well.
2. In a large-sized bowl, add remaining ingredients and mix well.
3. Add oil mixture and mix until well blended.
4. Place the mixture into a baking dish.
5. Select "AIRFRY/SUPER CONVECTION" of Breville Smart Oven Air Fryer Pro and adjust the temperature to 350 °F.
6. Adjust the time for 15 minutes and press "Start/Stop" to begin preheating.
7. As the unit beeps to show that it is preheated, arrange the baking dish over the wire rack.
8. While cooking, stir the granola after every 5 minutes.
9. After cooking time is finished, remove the baking dish from oven.
10. Set the baking dish of granola aside to cool completely before serving.

Per Serving:
Calories: 302| Fat: 16.1g| Carbs: 35.1g| Fiber: 5.7g| Protein: 6.9g

PUMPKIN PORRIDGE

Prep Time: 10 mins.| Cook Time: 5 hrs.| Serves: 8

- ✓ 1 C. unsweetened almond milk, divided
- ✓ 2 lb. pumpkin, peeled and cubed into ½-inch size
- ✓ 6-8 drops liquid stevia
- ✓ ½ tsp. ground allspice
- ✓ 1 tbsp. ground cinnamon
- ✓ 1 tsp. ground nutmeg
- ✓ ½ C. walnuts, chopped

1. In an oven-safe pan that will fit in the Breville Smart Oven Air Fryer Pro,

place ½ C. of almond milk, pumpkin, stevia and spices and stir to combine.
2. Cover the pan with a lid.
3. Arrange the pan over the wire rack.
4. Select "SLOW COOK" of Breville Smart Oven Air Fryer Pro and set on "Low".
5. Adjust the time for 5 hours and press "Start/Stop" to begin cooking.
6. After cooking time is finished, remove the pan from oven.
7. Remove the lid of pan and stir in the remaining almond milk.
8. Serve warm with the topping of walnuts.

Per Serving:
Calories: 96| Fat: 5.5g| Carbs: 11.2g| Fiber: 4.5g| Protein: 3.3g

THREE GRAINS PORRIDGE
Prep Time: 10 mins.| Cook Time: 7 hrs.| Serves: 10

✓ ¾ C. pearl barley
✓ ¾ C. steel-cut oats
✓ ½ C. uncooked quinoa, rinsed
✓ 6 C. unsweetened almond milk
✓ 2 C. coconut water
✓ ¼ C. maple syrup
✓ 1½ tsp. pure vanilla extract
✓ ¼ tsp. salt

1. In an oven-safe pan that will fit in the Breville Smart Oven Air Fryer Pro, place all ingredients and stir to combine.
2. Cover the pan with a lid.

3. Arrange the pan over the wire rack.
4. Select "SLOW COOK" of Breville Smart Oven Air Fryer Pro and set on "Low".
5. Adjust the time for 7 hours and press "Start/Stop" to begin cooking.
6. After cooking time is finished, remove the pan from oven.
7. Remove the lid of pan and stir the mixture well.
8. Serve warm.

Per Serving:
Calories: 188| Fat: 3.8g| Carbs: 33.6g| Fiber: 5.3g| Protein: 5.4g

CHEESE TOASTS WITH SALMON
Prep Time: 10 mins.| Cook Time: 4 mins.| Serves: 2

✓ 4 whole-wheat bread slices
✓ 1 garlic clove, minced
✓ 8 oz. ricotta cheese
✓ 1 tsp. lemon zest
✓ Freshly ground black pepper, as required
✓ 4 oz. smoked salmon

1. In a food processor, add the garlic, ricotta, lemon zest and black pepper and pulse until smooth.
2. Spread the ricotta mixture over each bread slices evenly.
3. Arrange the bread slices in the air fryer basket.
4. Select "TOAST" of Breville Smart Oven Air Fryer Pro and then adjust the temperature to 355 °F.
5. Adjust the time for 4 minutes and press "Start/Stop" to begin preheating.
6. As the unit beeps to show that it is preheated, insert the air fryer basket in the oven.
7. After cooking time is finished, remove the air fryer basket from oven and transfer the bread slices onto serving plates.
8. Top each slice with salmon and serve.

Per Serving:
Calories: 274 | Fat: 12g | Carbs: 15.7g | Fiber: 0.5g | Protein: 24.8g

CLOUD EGGS

Prep Time: 10 mins. | Cook Time: 15 mins. | Serves: 4

- ✓ Non-stick cooking spray
- ✓ 4 eggs, whites and yolks separated
- ✓ Pinch of salt
- ✓ Pinch of freshly ground black pepper
- ✓ 4 whole-wheat bread slices, toasted

1. Line a baking dish with parchment paper and then grease it with cooking spray.
2. In a bowl, add the egg white, salt and black pepper and beat until stiff peaks form.
3. Dollop 4 large spoonfuls of the whipped egg whites onto the prepared baking sheet.
4. With the back of a spoon, make a small well in the middle of each eff mound.
5. Select "BROIL" of Breville Smart Oven Air Fryer Pro and adjust the time for 7 minutes and press "Start/Stop" to begin preheating.
6. As the unit beeps to show that it is preheated, arrange the baking dish over the wire rack.
7. After 5 minutes of cooking, place 1 egg yolk into each egg whites pocket.
8. After cooking time is finished, remove the baking dish from oven.

9. Transfer the eggs onto serving plates and serve alongside toasted bread slices.

Per Serving:
Calories: 87 | Fat: 4.7g | Carbs: 4.9g | Fiber: 0.2g | Protein: 6.2g

SPINACH & EGGS TART

Prep Time: 15 mins. | Cook Time: 25 mins. | Serves: 4

- ✓ Non-stick cooking spray
- ✓ 1 puff pastry sheet, cut into a 9x13-inch rectangle
- ✓ 4 eggs
- ✓ ½ C. cheddar cheese, grated
- ✓ 7 cooked thick-cut bacon strips
- ✓ ½ C. cooked spinach
- ✓ 1 egg, lightly beaten

1. Lightly grease the enamel roasting pan of Breville Smart Oven Air Fryer Pro with cooking spray. Set aside.
2. Arrange the pastry into the prepared roasting pan.
3. With a small knife, gently cut a 1-inch border around the edges of the puff pastry without cutting all the way through.
4. With a fork, pierce the center of the pastry a few times.
5. Select "BAKE" of oven and adjust the temperature to 400 °F.
6. Adjust the time for 10 minutes and press "Start/Stop" to begin preheating.
7. As the unit beeps to show that it is preheated, insert the roasting pan in the oven.
8. After cooking time is finished, remove the roasting pan from oven and sprinkle the cheese onto the center of pastry.
9. Place the spinach and bacon in an even layer across the tart.
10. Now, crack the eggs, leaving space between each one.
11. Select "BAKE" of Breville Smart Oven

Air Fryer Pro and adjust the temperature to 400 °F.

12. Adjust the time for 15 minutes and press "Start/Stop" to begin preheating.

13. Insert the roasting pan in the oven.

14. After cooking time is finished, remove the roasting pan from oven and set aside to cool for 2-3 minutes before cutting.

15. With a pizza cutter, cut into 4 portions and serve.

Per Serving:
Calories: 231| Fat: 17.4g| Carbs: 5.7g| Fiber: 0.3g| Protein: 13.8g

CHICKEN & ZUCCHINI OMELET

Prep Time: 15 mins.| Cook Time: 35 mins.| Serves: 6

- ✓ Non-stick cooking spray
- ✓ 8 eggs
- ✓ ½ C. unsweetened almond milk
- ✓ 1/8 tsp. red pepper flakes, crushed
- ✓ Salt and ground black pepper, as required
- ✓ 1 C. cooked chicken, chopped
- ✓ 1 C. Monterrey Jack cheese, shredded
- ✓ ½ C. scallion, chopped
- ✓ ¾ C. zucchini, chopped

1. Lightly grease a baking dish with cooking spray. Set aside.

2. In a large-sized bowl, add eggs, almond milk, salt and black pepper and whisk well.

3. Add remaining ingredients and stir to combine.

4. Place the omelet mixture into the prepared baking dish.

5. Select "BAKE" of Breville Smart Oven Air Fryer Pro and adjust the temperature to 315 °F.

6. Adjust the time for 35 minutes and press "Start/Stop" to begin preheating.

7. As the unit beeps to show that it is preheated, arrange the baking dish over the wire rack.

8. After cooking time is finished, remove the baking dish from oven and place onto a cooling rack to cool for about 5 minutes before serving.

9. Cut into equal-sized wedges and serve.

Per Serving:
Calories: 209| Fat: 13.3g| Carbs: 2.3g| Fiber: 0.3g| Protein: 9.8g

BACON & KALE FRITTATA

Prep Time: 10 mins.| Cook Time: 20 mins.| Serves: 4

- ✓ ½ C. bacon, chopped
- ✓ ½ C. fresh kale, tough ribs removed and chopped
- ✓ 1 tomato, cubed
- ✓ 6 eggs
- ✓ Salt and ground black pepper, as required
- ✓ ½ C. Parmesan cheese, grated

1. Heat a non-stick skillet over medium heat and cook the bacon for about 5 minutes.

2. Add the kale and cook for about 1-2 minutes.

3. Add the tomato and cook for about 2-3 minutes.

4. Remove from the heat and drain the grease from skillet.

5. Set aside to cool slightly.

6. Meanwhile, in a small bowl, add the eggs, salt and black pepper and beat well.

7. In a greased baking dish, place the bacon mixture and top with the eggs, followed by the cheese.

8. Select "AIRFRY/SUPER CONVECTION" of Breville Smart Oven Air Fryer Pro and then adjust the temperature to 355 °F.

9. Adjust the time for 10 minutes and press "Start/Stop" to begin preheating.

10. As the unit beeps to show that it is

preheated, arrange the baking dish over the wire rack

11. After cooking time is finished, remove the baking dish from oven and place onto a cooling rack to cool for about 5 minutes before serving.

12. Cut into 4 wedges and serve.

Per Serving:
Calories: 293 | Fat: 19.7g | Carbs: 3.4g | Fiber: 0.3g | Protein: 25.4g

SAUSAGE & MUSHROOM CASSEROLE

Prep Time: 15 mins. | Cook Time: 19 mins. | Serves: 6

- ✓ 1 tbsp. olive oil
- ✓ ½ lb. spicy ground sausage
- ✓ ¾ C. yellow onion, chopped
- ✓ 5 fresh mushrooms, slice
- ✓ 8 eggs, beaten
- ✓ ½ tsp. garlic salt
- ✓ ¾ C. cheddar cheese, shredded and divided
- ✓ ¼ C. alfredo sauce

1. In a non-stick wok, heat oil over medium heat and cook the sausage and onion for about 4-5 minutes
2. Add in the sliced mushrooms and cook for about 6-7 minutes
3. Remove from oven and drain the grease from the wok.
4. In a bowl, add sausage mixture, beaten eggs, garlic salt, ½ C. of cheese and Alfredo sauce and stir to combine.
5. Place the sausage mixture into a baking dish.
6. Select "AIRFRY/SUPER CONVECTION" of Breville Smart Oven Air Fryer Pro and then adjust the temperature to 390 °F.
7. Adjust the time for 12 minutes and press "Start/Stop" to begin preheating.

8. As the unit beeps to show that it is preheated, arrange the baking dish over the wire rack.
9. After 6 minutes of cooking, stir the sausage mixture well.
10. After cooking, remove the baking dish from the oven and place onto a cooling rack to cool for about 5 minutes before serving.
11. Cut the casserole into equal-sized wedges and serve with the topping of remaining cheese.

Per Serving:
Calories: 319 | Fat: 24.5g | Carbs: 5g | Fiber: 0.5g | Protein: 19.7g

EGGS WITH TURKEY

Prep Time: 10 mins. | Cook Time: 30 mins. | Serves: 4

- ✓ Non-stick cooking spray
- ✓ 1 tbsp. unsalted butter
- ✓ 1 lb. fresh baby spinach
- ✓ 4 eggs
- ✓ 7 oz. cooked turkey, chopped
- ✓ 4 tsp. whole milk
- ✓ Salt and ground black pepper, as required

1. Grease 4 ramekins with cooking spray. Set aside.
2. In a non-stick wok, melt butter over medium heat and cook the spinach for about 2-3 minutes or until just wilted.
3. Remove the wok of spinach from heat and transfer the spinach into a bowl.
4. Set aside to cool slightly.
5. Divide the spinach into the prepared ramekins, followed by the turkey.
6. Crack 1 egg into each ramekin and drizzle with milk.
7. Sprinkle with salt and black pepper.
8. Select "AIRFRY/SUPER CONVECTION" of Breville Smart Oven Air Fryer Pro and then adjust the temperature to 355 °F.

9. Adjust the time for 20 minutes and press "Start/Stop" to begin preheating.
10. As the unit beeps to show that it is preheated, arrange the ramekins over the wire rack.
11. After cooking time is finished, remove the ramekins from oven and place onto a cooling rack to cool for about 5 minutes before serving.

Per Serving:
Calories: 201 | Fat: 10.3g | Carbs: 4.7g | Fiber: 2.5g | Protein: 23.5g

PUMPKIN PANCAKES
Prep Time: 10 mins. | Cook Time: 12 mins. | Serves: 4

- ✓ Non-stick cooking spray
- ✓ 1 square puff pastry
- ✓ 3 tbsp. pumpkin filling
- ✓ 1 small egg, beaten

1. Grease the enamel roasting pan of Breville Smart Oven Air Fryer Pro with cooking spray. Set aside.
2. Roll out a puff pastry square and layer it with pumpkin pie filling, leaving about ¼-inch space around the edges.
3. Cut it up into 8 equal-sized square pieces and coat the edges with beaten egg.
4. Arrange the squares into the greased roasting pan.
5. Select "AIRFRY/SUPER CONVECTION" of Breville Smart Oven Air Fryer Pro and then adjust the temperature to 355 °F.
6. Adjust the time for 12 minutes and press "Start/Stop" to begin preheating.
7. As the unit beeps to show that it is preheated, insert the roasting pan in the oven.
8. After cooking time is finished, remove the roasting pan from oven.
9. Serve warm.

Per Serving:

Calories: 109 | Fat: 6.7g | Carbs: 9.8g | Fiber: 0.5g | Protein: 2.4g

CRANBERRY OATS MUFFINS
Prep Time: 15 mins. | Cook Time: 10 mins. | Serves: 8

- ✓ Non-stick cooking spray
- ✓ ½ C. all-purpose flour
- ✓ ¼ C. rolled oats
- ✓ 1/8 tsp. baking powder
- ✓ ½ C. powdered sugar
- ✓ ½ C. unsalted butter, softened
- ✓ 2 egg
- ✓ ¼ tsp. vanilla extract
- ✓ ¼ C. dried cranberries

1. Grease 4 muffin molds with cooking spray. Set aside.
2. In a bowl, mix together the flour, oats, and baking powder.
3. In another bowl, add the sugar and butter. Beat until you get the creamy texture.
4. Then, add in the egg and vanilla extract and beat until well combined.
5. Add the egg mixture into oat mixture and mix until just combined.
6. Fold in the cranberries.
7. Place the mixture into the prepared muffin molds evenly.
8. Select "AIRFRY/SUPER CONVECTION" of Breville Smart Oven Air Fryer Pro and then adjust the temperature to 355 °F.

9. Adjust the time for 10 minutes and press "Start/Stop" to begin preheating.
10. As the unit beeps to show that it is preheated, arrange the muffin C. over the wire rack.
11. After cooking time is finished, remove the muffin molds from oven and place onto a cooling rack to cool for at least 8-10 minutes.
12. Then invert the muffins onto the cooling rack to cool completely before serving.

Per Serving:
Calories: 187 | Fat: 12.9g | Carbs: 15.6g | Fiber: 0.6g | Protein: 2.7g

HAM & CREAM MUFFINS
Prep Time: 10 mins. | Cook Time: 18 mins. | Serves: 6

- ✓ Non-stick cooking spray
- ✓ 6 ham slices
- ✓ 6 eggs
- ✓ 6 tbsp. heavy cream
- ✓ 3 tbsp. mozzarella cheese, shredded
- ✓ ¼ tsp. dried basil, crushed

1. Grease 6 C. of a muffin tin with cooking spray.
2. Line each prepared muffin C. with 1 ham slice.
3. Crack 1 egg into each muffin C. and top with cream.
4. Sprinkle with cheese and basil.
5. Select "AIRFRY/SUPER CONVECTION" of Breville Smart Oven Air Fryer Pro and then adjust the temperature to 350 °F.
6. Adjust the time for 18 minutes and press "Start/Stop" to begin preheating.
7. As the unit beeps to show that it is preheated, arrange the muffin tin over the wire rack.
8. After cooking time is finished, remove the muffin tin from oven and place onto

a cooling rack to cool for at least 8-10 minutes.
9. Then invert the muffins onto the platter and serve warm.

Per Serving:
Calories: 156 | Fat: 10g | Carbs: 2.3g | Fiber: 0.4g | Protein: 14.3g

YOGURT BREAD
Prep Time: 20 mins. | Cook Time: 40 mins. | Serves: 10

- ✓ Non-stick cooking spray
- ✓ 1½ C. warm water, divided
- ✓ 1½ tsp. active dry yeast
- ✓ 1 tsp. white sugar
- ✓ 3 C. all-purpose flour
- ✓ 1 C. plain Greek yogurt
- ✓ 2 tsp. kosher salt

1. In the bowl of a stand mixer, attached with a dough hook attachment, add ½ C. of warm water, yeast and sugar and mix well.
2. Set aside for about 5 minutes.
3. Add flour, yogurt, and salt and mix on medium-low speed until the dough comes together.
4. Then mix on medium speed for 5 minutes.
5. Place the dough into a bowl.
6. With plastic wrap, cover the bowl and place in a warm place for about 2-3 hours or until doubled in size.

7. Line a wire rack with parchment paper and then grease it with cooking spray. Set aside

8. Remove the dough from the bowl and place onto a lightly floured surface.

9. With your hands, shape the dough into a smooth ball.

10. Place the dough onto the prepared rack.

11. With a kitchen towel, cover the dough and let rest for 15 minutes.

12. With a very sharp knife, cut a 4x½-inch deep cut down the center of the dough.

13. Select "ROAST" of Breville Smart Oven Air Fryer Pro and adjust the temperature to 325 °F.

14. Adjust the time for 40 minutes and press "Start/Stop" to begin preheating

15. As the unit beeps to show that it is preheated, arrange the dough over the wire rack.

16. After cooking time is finished, remove the bread from oven and place onto a cooling rack to cool completely before slicing

17. Cut the bread into desired-sized slices and serve.

Per Serving:
Calories: 157 | Fat: 0.7g | Carbs: 31g | Fiber: 1.1g | Protein: 5.5g

APPLE & ZUCCHINI BREAD
Prep Time: 15 mins. | Cook Time: 30 mins. | Serves: 8

✓ Non-stick cooking spray
For Bread:
✓ 1 C. all-purpose flour
✓ ¾ tsp. baking powder
✓ ¼ tsp. baking soda
✓ 1¼ tsp. ground cinnamon
✓ ¼ tsp. salt
✓ 1/3 C. vegetable oil
✓ 1/3 C. white sugar
✓ 1 egg
✓ 1 tsp. vanilla extract

✓ ½ C. zucchini, shredded
✓ ½ C. apple, cored and shredded
✓ 5 tbsp. walnuts, chopped

For Topping:
✓ 1 tbsp. walnuts, chopped
✓ 2 tsp. brown sugar
✓ ¼ tsp. ground cinnamon

1. Lightly grease a loaf pan with cooking spray. Set aside

2. For bread: in a bowl, blend together the flour, baking powder, baking soda, cinnamon, and salt

3. In another large-sized bowl, add oil, sugar, egg, and vanilla extract and mix well.

4. In the bowl of oil mixture, add flour mixture and mix until just blended.

5. Gently fold in the zucchini, apple and walnuts.

6. For the topping: in a small-sized bowl, add all ingredients and whisk them well.

7. Place the bread mixture into the prepared loaf pan and sprinkle with the topping mixture.

8. Select "AIRFRY/SUPER CONVECTION" of Breville Smart Oven Air Fryer Pro and then adjust the temperature to 325 °F.

9. Adjust the time for 30 minutes and press "Start/Stop" to begin preheating

10. As the unit beeps to show that it is preheated, arrange the loaf pan over the wire rack.

11. After cooking time is finished, remove the loaf pan from oven and place the pan onto a wire rack to cool for about 10 minutes.

12. Then turn the bread onto the cooling rack to cool completely before slicing.

13. Cut the bread into desired-sized slices and serve.

Per Serving:
Calories: 225 | Fat: 13.3g | Carbs: 24g | Fiber: 1.7g | Protein: 3.9g

POULTRY RECIPES

HERBED WHOLE CHICKEN
Prep Time: 15 mins.| Cook Time: 1 hr.|
Serves: 8

- ✓ 1 tbsp. fresh basil, chopped
- ✓ 1 tbsp. fresh oregano, chopped
- ✓ 1 tbsp. fresh thyme, chopped
- ✓ Salt and ground black pepper, as required
- ✓ 1 (4½-lb.) whole chicken, necks and giblets removed
- ✓ 3 tbsp. olive oil, divided

1. Grease the air fryer basket of Breville Smart Oven Air Fryer Pro with cooking spray.
2. In a bowl, blend together the herbs, salt and black pepper.
3. Coat the chicken with 2 tbsp. of oil and then rub inside, outside and underneath the skin with half of the herb mixture generously.
4. Arrange the chicken into the prepared air fryer basket, breast-side down.
5. Select "AIRFRY/SUPER CONVECTION" of oven and then adjust the temperature to 360 °F.
6. Adjust the time for 60 minutes and press "Start/Stop" to begin preheating.
7. As the unit beeps to show that it is preheated, insert the air fryer basket in the oven.

8. After 30 minutes of cooking, arrange the chicken, breast-side up and oat with the remaining oil.
9. Then rub with the remaining herb mixture.
10. After cooking time is finished, remove the air fryer basket from oven and place the chicken onto a cutting board for about 10 minutes before carving.
11. Cut the chicken into desired-sized pieces and serve.

Per Serving:
Calories: 435 | Fat: 213.26.6g | Carbs: 1g |
Fiber: 0.5g | Protein: 74.2g

SPICY CHICKEN LEGS
Prep Time: 10 mins.| Cook Time: 25
mins.| Serves: 6

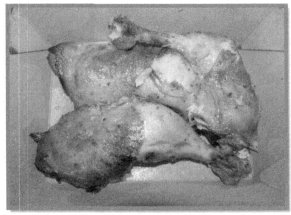

- ✓ Non-stick cooking spray
- ✓ 2½ lb. chicken legs
- ✓ 2 tbsp. olive oil
- ✓ 1 tsp. smoked paprika
- ✓ 1 tsp. garlic powder
- ✓ ½ tsp. ground cumin
- ✓ Salt and ground black pepper, as required

1. Grease the enamel roasting pan of Breville Smart Oven Air Fryer Pro with cooking spray. Set aside.

2. Arrange the chicken legs into the prepared roasting pan.
3. Select "AIRFRY/SUPER CONVECTION" of oven and then adjust the temperature to 400 °F.
4. Adjust the time for 25 minutes and press "Start/Stop" to begin preheating.
5. As the unit beeps to show that it is preheated, insert the roasting pan in the oven.
6. After cooking time is finished, remove the roasting pan from oven and transfer the chicken pieces onto a platter.
7. Serve hot.

Per Serving:
Calories: 402| Fat: 18.8g| Carbs: 0.6g| Fiber: 0.2g| Protein: 54.8g

HERBED CHICKEN DRUMSTICKS
Prep Time: 10 mins.| Cook Time: 20 mins.| Serves: 4

✓ Non-stick cooking spray
✓ 2 tbsp. olive oil
✓ 1 tsp. dried thyme, crushed
✓ ½ tsp. dried rosemary, crushed
✓ ½ tsp. dried oregano, crushed
✓ Salt and ground black pepper, as required
✓ 4 (6-oz.) chicken drumsticks

1. Grease the enamel roasting pan of Breville Smart Oven Air Fryer Pro with cooking spray. Set aside.

2. In a large-sized bowl, place the oil, herbs, salt and black pepper and mix well.
3. Add chicken drumsticks and coat with the mixture generously.
4. Place the chicken drumsticks into the prepared roasting pan.
5. Select "AIRFRY/SUPER CONVECTION" of oven and then adjust the temperature to 375 °F.
6. Adjust the time for 20 minutes and press "Start/Stop" to begin preheating.
8. As the unit beeps to show that it is preheated, insert the roasting pan in the oven.
7. After cooking time is finished, remove the baking pan from oven and transfer the chicken drumsticks onto plates.
8. Serve hot.

Per Serving:
Calories: 349| Fat: 16.8g| Carbs: 0.3g| Fiber: 0.2g| Protein: 46.8g

BUTTERED CHICKEN THIGHS
Prep Time: 10 mins.| Cook Time: 20 mins.| Serves: 2

✓ Non-stick cooking spray
✓ 2 (4-oz.) skinless, boneless chicken thighs
✓ Salt and ground black pepper, as required
✓ 2 tbsp. unsalted butter, melted

1. Grease the enamel roasting pan of Breville Smart Oven Air Fryer Pro with cooking spray. Set aside.
2. Rub the chicken thighs with salt and black pepper evenly and then brush with melted butter.
3. Place the chicken thighs into the prepared roasting pan.
4. Select "BAKE" of oven and adjust the temperature to 450 °F.
5. Adjust the time for 20 minutes and press "Start/Stop" to begin preheating.

9. As the unit beeps to show that it is preheated, insert the roasting pan in the oven.
6. After cooking time is finished, remove the roasting pan from oven and transfer the chicken thighs onto plates.
7. Serve hot.

Per Serving:
Calories: 193 | Fat: 9.8g | Carbs: 0g | Fiber: 0g | Protein: 25.4g

MARINATED CHICKEN THIGHS
Prep Time: 10 mins. | Cook Time: 30 mins. | Serves: 4

- ✓ 4 (6-oz.) bone-in, skin-on chicken thighs
- ✓ Salt and ground black pepper, as required
- ✓ ½ C. Italian salad dressing
- ✓ 1 tsp. onion powder
- ✓ 1 tsp. garlic powder

1. Season the chicken thighs with salt and black pepper evenly.
2. In a large-sized bowl, add chicken thighs and dressing and mix well.
3. Grease the air fryer basket of Breville Smart Oven Air Fryer Pro with cooking spray.
4. With plastic wrap, cover the bowl of chicken thighs and refrigerate to marinate overnight.
5. Remove the chicken thighs from the bowl and place onto a plate.
6. Sprinkle the chicken thighs with onion powder and garlic powder.
7. Arrange the chicken thighs into the prepared air fryer basket.
8. Select "AIRFRY/SUPER CONVECTION" of oven and then adjust the temperature to 360 °F.
9. Adjust the time for 30 minutes and press "Start/Stop" to begin preheating.
10. As the unit beeps to show that it is preheated, insert the air fryer basket in the oven.

11. Flip the chicken thighs once halfway through.
12. After cooking time is finished, remove the air fryer basket from oven and transfer the chicken thighs onto serving plates.
13. Serve hot.

Per Serving:
Calories: 286 | Fat: 5.2g | Carbs: 4.1g | Fiber: 0.1g | Protein: 33.4g

SPICED CHICKEN BREASTS
Prep Time: 10 mins. | Cook Time: 35 mins. | Serves: 4

- ✓ 1½ tbsp. smoked paprika
- ✓ 1 tsp. ground cumin
- ✓ Salt and ground black pepper, as required
- ✓ 2 (12-oz.) bone-in, skin-on chicken breasts
- ✓ 1 tbsp. olive oil

1. Grease the air fryer basket of Breville Smart Oven Air Fryer Pro. Set aside.
2. In a small-sized bowl, blend together the paprika, cumin, salt and black pepper.
3. Coat the chicken breasts with oil evenly and then season with the spice mixture generously.
4. Arrange the chicken breasts into the prepared air fryer basket.
5. Select "AIRFRY/SUPER CONVECTION" of oven and then adjust the temperature to 375 °F.
6. Adjust the time for 35 minutes and press "Start/Stop" to begin preheating.
7. As the unit beeps to show that it is preheated, insert the air fryer basket in the oven.
8. While cooking, flip the chicken thighs once halfway through.
9. After cooking time is finished, remove the air fryer basket from oven and

transfer the chicken breasts onto a cutting board.

10. Cut each breast in 2 equal-sized pieces and serve.

Per Serving:
Calories: 363 | Fat: 16.6g | Carbs: 1.7g | Fiber: 1g | Protein: 49.7g

BREADED CHICKEN BREASTS
Prep Time: 15 mins. | Cook Time: 12 mins. | Serves: 6

- ✓ 1 C. panko breadcrumbs
- ✓ ½ C. Parmesan cheese, grated
- ✓ ¼ C. fresh rosemary, minced
- ✓ ¼ tsp. cayenne powder
- ✓ Salt and ground black pepper, as required
- ✓ 6 (4-oz.) boneless, skinless chicken breasts
- ✓ 3 tbsp. olive oil
- ✓ Non-stick cooking spray

1. In a shallow dish, add breadcrumbs, Parmesan cheese, rosemary, cayenne powder, salt and black pepper and mix well.
2. Rub each chicken breast with oil evenly and then coat with the breadcrumb mixture.
3. Arrange the chicken breasts into the enamel roasting pan and spray with cooking spray.
4. Select "AIRFRY/SUPER CONVECTION" of Breville Smart Oven Air Fryer Pro and then adjust the temperature to 350 °F.
5. Adjust the time for 12 minutes and press "Start/Stop" to begin preheating.
6. As the unit beeps to show that it is preheated, insert the roasting pan in the oven.
7. While cooking, flip the chicken breasts once halfway through.

8. After cooking time is finished, remove the roasting pan from oven and transfer the chicken breasts onto serving plates.
9. Serve hot.

Per Serving:
Calories: 305 | Fat: 3.2g | Carbs: 4.3g | Fiber: 1.1g | Protein: 30.9g

CHICKEN CORDON BLEU
Prep Time: 15 mins. | Cook Time: 25 mins. | Serves: 2

- ✓ Non-stick cooking spray
- ✓ 2 (6-oz.) boneless, skinless chicken breast halves, pounded into ¼-inch thickness
- ✓ 2 (¾-oz.) deli ham slices
- ✓ 2 Swiss cheese slices
- ✓ ½ C. all-purpose flour
- ✓ 1/8 tsp. paprika
- ✓ Salt and ground black pepper, as required
- ✓ 1 large egg
- ✓ 2 tbsp. 2% milk
- ✓ ½ C. seasoned breadcrumbs
- ✓ 1 tbsp. olive oil
- ✓ 1 tbsp. unsalted butter, melted

1. Grease a baking dish with cooking spray. Set aside.
2. Arrange the chicken breast halves onto a smooth surface.
3. Arrange 1 ham slice over each chicken breast half, followed by the cheese.

4. Roll up each chicken breast half and tuck in ends.
5. With toothpicks, secure the rolls.
6. In a shallow plate, blend together the flour, paprika, salt and black pepper.
7. In a shallow bowl, place the egg and milk and whisk slightly.
8. In a third shallow plate, place the breadcrumbs.
9. Coat each chicken roll with flour mixture, then dip into egg mixture and finally coat with breadcrumbs.
10. In a small wok, heat oil over medium heat and cook the chicken rolls for about 3-5 minutes or until browned from all sides.
11. Transfer the chicken rolls into the prepared baking dish.
12. Select "BAKE" of Breville Smart Oven Air Fryer Pro and adjust the temperature to 350 °F.
13. Adjust the time for 25 minutes and press "Start/Stop" to begin preheating.
14. As the unit beeps to show that it is preheated, arrange the baking dish over the wire rack.
15. After cooking time is finished, remove the baking dish from oven and transfer the chicken breasts onto a serving platter.
16. Discard the toothpicks and drizzle the chicken rolls with melted butter.
17. Serve immediately.

Per Serving:
Calories: 672 | Fat: 28g | Carbs: 45.9g | Fiber: 2.4g | Protein: 56.2g

CHICKEN & SPINACH SOUP
Prep Time: 15 mins. | Cook Time: 6 hrs. | Serves: 6

✓ 2 tbsp. unsalted butter, melted
✓ 4 C. cooked chicken, chopped
✓ 8 C. fresh spinach, chopped
✓ 1 large carrot, peeled and chopped
✓ 1 small onion, chopped finely
✓ ½ tbsp. garlic, minced
✓ Salt and ground black pepper, as required
✓ 6 C. chicken broth

1. In an oven-safe pan that will fit in the Breville Smart Oven Air Fryer Pro, place all ingredients and stir to combine.
2. Cover the pan with a lid.
3. Arrange the pan over the wire rack.
4. Select "SLOW COOK" of Breville Smart Oven Air Fryer Pro and set on "Low".
5. Adjust the time for 6 hours and press "Start/Stop" to begin cooking.
6. After cooking time is finished, remove the pan from oven.
7. Remove the lid of pan and serve hot.

Per Serving:
Calories: 233 | Fat: 8.2g | Carbs: 4.9g | Fiber: 1.4g | Protein: 33.4g

CHICKEN KABOBS
Prep Time: 15 mins. | Cook Time: 9 mins. | Serves: 2

✓ 2 (4-oz.) skinless, boneless chicken breasts, cut into medium-sized pieces
✓ 1 tbsp. fresh lemon juice

- ✓ 3 garlic cloves, grated
- ✓ 1 tbsp. fresh oregano, minced
- ✓ ½ tsp. lemon zest, grated
- ✓ Salt and ground black pepper, as required
- ✓ 1 tsp. plain Greek yogurt
- ✓ 1 tsp. olive oil

1. Grease the air fryer basket of Breville Smart Oven Air Fryer Pro. Set aside.
2. In a large-sized bowl, add chicken, lemon juice, garlic, oregano, lemon zest, salt and black pepper and toss to coat well.
3. Cover the bowl and refrigerate overnight.
4. Remove the bowl from refrigerator and stir in the yogurt and oil.
5. Thread the coated chicken pieces onto metal skewers.
6. Arrange the skewers into the prepared air fryer basket.
7. Select "AIRFRY/SUPER CONVECTION" of oven and then adjust the temperature to 350 °F.
8. Adjust the time for 9 minutes and press "Start/Stop" to begin preheating.
9. As the unit beeps to show that it is preheated, insert the air fryer basket in the oven.
10. Flip the skewers once halfway through.
11. After cooking time is finished, remove the air fryer basket from oven and transfer the kabobs onto a serving platter.
12. Serve hot.

Per Serving:
Calories: 344| Fat: 15.9g| Carbs: 3.7g| Fiber: 0.6g| Protein: 45g

ROSEMARY TURKEY LEGS
Prep Time: 10 mins.| Cook Time: 30 mins.| Serves: 2

- ✓ 2 garlic cloves, minced

- ✓ 1 tbsp. fresh rosemary, minced
- ✓ 1 tsp. fresh lime zest, finely grated
- ✓ 2 tbsp. olive oil
- ✓ 1 tbsp. fresh lime juice
- ✓ Salt and ground black pepper, as required
- ✓ 2 turkey legs

1. In a large-sized bowl, blend together the garlic, rosemary, lime zest, oil, lime juice, salt, and black pepper
2. Add turkey legs and generously coat with marinade.
3. Refrigerate to marinate for about 6-8 hours.
4. Grease the air fryer basket of Breville Smart Oven Air Fryer Pro with cooking spray.
5. Place turkey legs into the prepared air fryer basket.
6. Select "AIRFRY/SUPER CONVECTION" of oven and then adjust the temperature to 350 °F.
7. Adjust the time for 30 minutes and press "Start/Stop" to begin preheating.
8. As the unit beeps to show that it is preheated, insert the air fryer basket in the oven.
9. Flip the turkey legs once halfway through
10. After cooking time is finished, remove the air fryer basket from oven and place the turkey legs onto the serving plates.
11. Serve hot.

Per Serving:
Calories: 411| Fats: 24.3g| Carbs: 2.3g| Fiber: 0.9g| Proteins: 47.8g

BUTTERED TURKEY BREAST
Prep Time: 10 mins.| Cook Time: 55 mins.| Serves: 6

- ✓ ¼ C. unsalted butter, softened
- ✓ 4 tbsp. fresh rosemary, chopped
- ✓ Salt and ground black pepper, as required
- ✓ 1 (4-lb.) bone-in, skin-on turkey breast
- ✓ 2 tbsp. olive oil

1. In a bowl, add butter, rosemary, salt and black pepper and mix well.
2. Rub the herb mixture under the skin evenly.
3. Coat the outside of turkey breast with oil.
4. Grease the enamel roasting pan of Breville Smart Oven Air Fryer Pro with cooking spray. Set aside.
5. Select "BAKE" of oven and adjust the temperature to 350 °F.
6. Adjust the time for 55 minutes and press "Start/Stop" to begin preheating.
9. As the unit beeps to show that it is preheated, insert the roasting pan in the oven.
7. After cooking time is finished, remove the roasting pan from oven and transfer the turkey breast onto a cutting board.
8. With a piece of foil, wrap the turkey breast for about 15-20 minutes before slicing.
9. Then cut the turkey breast into desired-sized slices and serve.

Per Serving:
Calories: 333| Fat: 37g| Carbs: 1.8g| Fiber: 1.1g| Protein: 65.1g

TURKEY BURGERS
Prep Time: 15 mins.| Cook Time: 8 mins.| Serves: 6

- ✓ Non-stick cooking spray
- ✓ 2 lb. ground turkey
- ✓ ½ tbsp. onion powder
- ✓ ½ tbsp. garlic powder
- ✓ ¼ tsp. ground cumin
- ✓ Salt and ground black pepper, as required
- ✓ 6 C. fresh baby arugula

1. Grease the enamel roasting pan of Breville Smart Oven Air Fryer Pro with cooking spray.
2. In a large-sized bowl, add all ingredients and mix well.
3. Make 6 equal-sized patties from the mixture.
4. Arrange the patties into the roasting pan in a single layer.
5. Select "AIRFRY/SUPER CONVECTION" of oven and then adjust the temperature to 360 °F.
6. Adjust the time for 8 minutes and press "Start/Stop" to begin preheating.
7. As the unit beeps to show that it is preheated, insert the roasting pan in the oven.
8. Flip the burgers once halfway through.
9. After cooking time is finished, remove the roasting pan from oven and transfer the burgers onto serving plates.
10. Serve hot alongside the arugula.

Per Serving:
Calories: 305| Fat: 16.8g| Carbs: 1.8g| Fiber: 0.4g| Protein: 42.1g

TURKEY WITH PUMPKIN
Prep Time: 15 mins.| Cook Time: 3 hrs.| Serves: 2

- ✓ 8 oz. turkey breast, chopped
- ✓ 3½ oz. pumpkin, peeled and chopped

- ✓ ½ of small yellow onion, chopped
- ✓ ½ tsp. ground cumin
- ✓ ½ tsp. ground cinnamon
- ✓ ¼ tsp. ground allspice
- ✓ Salt and ground black pepper, as required
- ✓ ½ C. chicken broth

1. Grease a Dutch oven that will fit in the Breville Smart Oven Air Fryer Pro.
2. In the prepared pan, place all the ingredients and stir to combine.
3. Arrange the Dutch oven over the wire rack.
4. Select "SLOW COOK" of Breville Smart Oven Air Fryer Pro and set on "High".
5. Adjust the time for 3 hours and press "Start/Stop" to begin cooking.
6. After cooking time is finished, remove the Dutch oven from oven.
7. Remove the lid of pan and serve hot.

Per Serving:
Calories: 155| Fat: 2.5g| Carbs: 11.5g| Fiber: 2.8g| Protein: 21.4g

TURKEY & BEANS CHILI
Prep Time: 15 mins.| Cook Time: 5 hrs. 10 mins.| Serves: 6

- ✓ 1 tbsp. olive oil
- ✓ 1 lb. lean ground turkey
- ✓ 1 red bell pepper, seeded and chopped
- ✓ 1 red onion, chopped finely
- ✓ 2 garlic cloves, minced
- ✓ 2 C. tomatoes, chopped finely
- ✓ 2 C. canned red kidney beans, rinsed
- ✓ 2 C. canned black beans, rinsed
- ✓ ½ C. tomato paste
- ✓ 1 tsp. ground cumin
- ✓ 1 tbsp. red chili powder
- ✓ ½ tsp. garlic powder
- ✓ Salt and ground black pepper, as required
- ✓ 1 C. chicken broth
- ✓ ½ C. fresh cilantro, chopped

1. In a Dutch oven that will fit in the Breville Smart Oven Air Fryer Pro, heat oil over medium heat and cook the turkey for about 4-5 minutes.
2. Add in bell pepper, onion and garlic and cook for about 3-5 minutes.
3. Remove the pan of turkey mixture from heat and stir in the remaining ingredients except for cilantro.
4. Arrange the Dutch oven over the wire rack.
5. Select "SLOW COOK" of Breville Smart Oven Air Fryer Pro and set on "Low".
6. Adjust the time for 5 hours and press "Start/Stop" to begin cooking.
7. After cooking time is finished, remove the Dutch oven from oven.
8. Remove the lid of pan and serve hot with the topping of cilantro.

Per Serving:
Calories: 457| Fat: 7.5g| Carbs: 64.8g| Fiber: 17.3g| Protein: 36.3g

RED MEAT RECIPES

BALSAMIC BEEF TOP ROAST
Prep Time: 10 mins. | Cook Time: 45 mins. | Serves: 10

- ✓ Non-stick cooking spray
- ✓ 1 tbsp. unsalted butter, melted
- ✓ 1 tbsp. balsamic vinegar
- ✓ ½ tsp. ground cumin
- ✓ ½ tsp. smoked paprika
- ✓ ½ tsp. red pepper flakes, crushed
- ✓ Salt and ground black pepper, as required
- ✓ 3 lb. beef top roast

1. Grease the enamel roasting pan of Breville Smart Oven Air Fryer Pro with cooking spray.
2. In a bowl, add butter, vinegar, spices, salt and black pepper and mix well.
3. Coat the roast with spice mixture generously.
4. With kitchen twines, tie the roast to keep it compact.
5. Arrange the roast into the roasting pan.
6. Select "AIRFRY/SUPER CONVECTION" of oven and then adjust the temperature to 360 °F.
7. Adjust the time for 45 minutes and press "Start/Stop" to begin preheating.
8. As the unit beeps to show that it is preheated, insert the roasting pan in the oven.
9. After cooking time is finished, remove the roasting pan from oven and place the roast onto a cutting board for about 10 minutes before slicing.
10. Cut the beef roast into desired-sized slices and serve.

Per Serving:
Calories: 305 | Fat: 17.2g | Carbs: 0.2g | Fiber: 0.1g | Protein: 35.1g

BACON-WRAPPED FILET MIGNON
Prep Time: 10 mins. | Cook Time: 15 mins. | Serves: 2

- ✓ 2 bacon slices
- ✓ 2 (4-oz.) filet mignon
- ✓ Salt and ground black pepper, as required
- ✓ Non-stick cooking spray

1. Wrap 1 bacon slice around each filet mignon and secure with toothpicks.
2. Season the filet mignon with salt and black pepper lightly.
3. Arrange the filet mignon onto the wire rack and spray with cooking spray.
4. Select "AIRFRY/SUPER CONVECTION" of Breville Smart Oven Air Fryer Pro and then adjust the temperature to 375 °F.
5. Adjust the time for 15 minutes and press "Start/Stop" to begin preheating.

6. As the unit beeps to show that it is preheated, insert the wire rack in the oven.
7. After cooking time is finished, remove the rack from oven.
8. Serve hot.

Per Serving:
Calories: 464| Fat: 23.6g| Carbs: 0.5g| Fiber: 0.1g| Protein: 58.5g

BRAISED BEEF SHANKS
Prep Time: 10 mins.| Cook Time: 6 hrs.| Serves: 4

- ✓ 2 lb. beef shanks
- ✓ 5 garlic cloves, minced
- ✓ 2 fresh rosemary sprigs
- ✓ 1 tbsp. fresh lime juice
- ✓ Salt and ground black pepper, as required
- ✓ 1 C. beef broth

1. Lightly grease a Dutch oven that will fit in the Breville Smart Oven Air Fryer Pro.
2. In the pan, add all ingredients and mix well.
3. Arrange the Dutch oven over the wire rack.
4. Select "SLOW COOK" of Breville Smart Oven Air Fryer Pro and set on "Low".
5. Adjust the time for 6 hours and press "Start/Stop" to begin cooking.
6. After cooking time is finished, remove the Dutch oven from oven.
7. Open the lid and serve hot.

Per Serving:
Calories: 471| Fat: 14.8g| Carbs: 1.5g| Fiber: 0.1g| Protein: 77.8g

BEEF & TOMATO CURRY
Prep Time: 10 mins.| Cook Time: 5 hrs.| Serves: 8

- ✓ 2 lb. beef stew meat, cubed

- ✓ 1½ C. fresh tomatoes, chopped finely
- ✓ 2 C. beef broth
- ✓ 1 C. unsweetened coconut milk
- ✓ Salt and ground black pepper, as required

1. In an oven-safe pan that will fit in the Breville Smart Oven Air Fryer Pro, place all ingredients and stir to combine.
2. Cover the pan with a lid.
3. Arrange the pan over the wire rack
4. Select "SLOW COOK" of Breville Smart Oven Air Fryer Pro and set on "High".
5. Adjust the time for 5 hours and press "Start/Stop" to begin cooking.
6. After cooking time is finished, remove the pan from oven.
7. Remove the lid of pan and stir the mixture well.
8. Serve hot.

Per Serving:
Calories: 526| Fat: 48.7g| Carbs: 3.2g| Fiber: 1.1g| Protein: 18.3g

BEEF JERKY
Prep Time: 15 mins.| Cook Time: 3 hrs.| Serves: 4

- ✓ 1½ lb. beef round roast, trimmed
- ✓ ½ C. Worcestershire sauce
- ✓ ½ C. low-sodium soy sauce
- ✓ 2 tsp. honey
- ✓ 1 tsp. liquid smoke
- ✓ 2 tsp. onion powder
- ✓ ½ tsp. red pepper flakes

✓ Ground black pepper, as required

1. In a zip-top bag, place the beef and freeze for 1-2 hours to firm up.
2. Arrange the beef onto a cutting board and cut against the grain into 1/8-¼-inch strips.
3. In a large-sized bowl, add remaining ingredients and mix until well blended.
4. Add beef slices and coat with the mixture generously
5. Refrigerate to marinate for about 4-6 hours.
6. Remove the beef slices from the bowl and with paper towels, pat dry them.
7. Divide the steak strips onto the oven racks of Breville Smart Oven Air Fryer Pro and arrange in an even layer.
8. Select "Dehydrate" of oven and adjust the temperature to 160 °F.
9. Adjust the time for 3 hours and press "Start/Stop" to begin preheating.
10. As the unit beeps to show that it is preheated, insert 1 rack in the top position and another in the center position.
11. After 1½ hours, switch the position of oven racks.
12. After cooking time is finished, remove the baking pans from oven.
13. Set the pans of beef slices aside to cool completely before serving.

Per Serving:
Calories: 341| Fat: 8.4g| Carbs: 12g|
Fiber: 0.2g| Protein: 51.6g

HERBED LEG OF LAMB
Prep Time: 10 mins.| Cook Time: 1¼ hrs.| Serves: 6

✓ 1 (2¼-lb.) boneless leg of lamb
✓ 3 tbsp. olive oil
✓ Salt and ground black pepper, as required
✓ 2 fresh rosemary sprigs
✓ 2 fresh thyme sprigs

1. Rub the leg of lamb with oil and sprinkle with salt and black pepper.
2. Wrap the leg of lamb with herb sprigs.
3. Arrange the leg of lamb into the prepared air fryer basket.
4. Select "AIRFRY/SUPER CONVECTION" of Breville Smart Oven Air Fryer Pro and then adjust the temperature to 300 °F.
5. Adjust the time for 75 minutes and press "Start/Stop" to begin preheating.
6. As the unit beeps to show that it is preheated, insert the air fryer basket in the oven.
7. After cooking time is finished, remove the air fryer basket from oven and place the leg of lamb onto a cutting board for about 10 minutes before slicing.
8. Cut the leg of lamb into desired-sized pieces and serve.

Per Serving:
Calories: 267| Fat: 12.9g| Carbs: 0g|
Fiber: 0g| Protein: 35.8g

CRUMBED RACK OF LAMB
Prep Time: 14 mins.| Cook Time: 30 mins.| Serves: 4

- ✓ 1 tbsp. unsalted butter, melted
- ✓ 1 garlic clove, finely chopped
- ✓ 1 (1¾-lb.) rack of lamb
- ✓ Salt and ground black pepper, as required
- ✓ 1 egg
- ✓ ½ C. panko breadcrumbs
- ✓ 1 tbsp. fresh thyme, minced
- ✓ 1 tbsp. fresh rosemary, minced

1. In a small-sized bowl, blend together the butter, garlic, salt, and black pepper.
2. Coat the rack of lamb with garlic mixture evenly.
3. In a shallow dish, beat the egg.
4. In another dish, blend together the breadcrumbs and herbs.
5. Dip the rack of lamb into beaten egg and then coat with breadcrumbs mixture.
6. Arrange the rack of lamb into the prepared air fryer basket.
7. Select "AIRFRY/SUPER CONVECTION" of Breville Smart Oven Air Fryer Pro and then adjust the temperature to 212 °F.
8. Adjust the time for 25 minutes and press "Start/Stop" to begin preheating.
9. As the unit beeps to show that it is preheated, insert the air fryer basket in the oven.
10. After 25 minutes of cooking, set the temperature of oven to 390 °F for 5 minutes.
11. After cooking time is finished, remove the air fryer basket from oven and place the rack onto a cutting board for at least 10 minutes.
12. Cut the rack into individual chops and serve.

Per Serving:
Calories: 429 | Fat: 22.7g | Carbs: 3.3g | Fiber: 0.7g | Protein: 42.3g

GLAZED LAMB CHOPS
Prep Time: 10 mins.| Cook Time: 15 mins.| Serves: 2

- ✓ Non-stick cooking spray
- ✓ 1 tbsp. Dijon mustard
- ✓ ½ tbsp. fresh lemon juice
- ✓ 1 tsp. maple syrup
- ✓ 1 tsp. canola oil
- ✓ ¼ tsp. red pepper flakes, crushed
- ✓ Salt and ground black pepper, as required
- ✓ 4 (4-oz.) lamb loin chops

1. Grease the enamel roasting pan of Breville Smart Oven Air Fryer Pro with cooking spray.
2. In a large-sized bowl, blend together the mustard, lemon juice, oil, maple syrup, red pepper flakes, salt and black pepper.
3. Add chops and coat with the mixture generously.
4. Place the chops into the greased roasting pan.
5. Select "BAKE" of oven and adjust the temperature to 390 °F.
6. Adjust the time for 15 minutes and press "Start/Stop" to begin preheating.
7. As the unit beeps to show that it is preheated, insert the roasting pan in the oven
8. Flip the chops once halfway through.
9. After cooking time is finished, remove the roasting pan from oven and transfer the chops onto plates.
10. Serve hot.

Per Serving:
Calories: 224| Fat: 9.1g| Carbs: 1.7g|
Fiber: 0.1g| Protein: 32g

LAMB & APRICOT CASSEROLE

Prep Time: 15 mins.| Cook Time: 8 hrs. 5 mins.| Serves: 4

- ✓ 1 tsp. ground cumin
- ✓ 1 tsp. ground coriander
- ✓ 1 tsp. ground cinnamon
- ✓ 1 tbsp. olive oil
- ✓ 1 lb. lamb shoulder, trimmed and cubed
- ✓ 1½ C. tomato paste
- ✓ 1 medium onion, chopped finely
- ✓ 2 garlic cloves, minced
- ✓ 1 C. dried apricots

1. In a bowl, blend together the spices.
2. Add lamb cubes and coat with the spice mixture evenly.
3. In a Dutch oven that will fit in the Breville Smart Oven Air Fryer Pro, heat oil over medium heat and cook the lamb cubes for about 4-5 minutes.
4. Remove the pan of lamb from heat and stir in the remaining ingredients.
5. Arrange the Dutch oven over the wire rack.
6. Select "SLOW COOK" of Breville Smart Oven Air Fryer Pro and set on "Low".
7. Adjust the time for 8 hours and press "Start/Stop" to begin cooking.
8. After cooking time is finished, remove the Dutch oven from oven and stir the mixture well.
9. Serve hot.

Per Serving:
Calories: 377| Fat: 0.5g| Carbs: 26.6g|
Fiber: 5.8g| Protein: 26.3g

HERBED LAMB MEATBALLS

Prep Time: 15 mins.| Cook Time: 7 hrs. 5 mins.| Serves: 8

- ✓ 2 lb. lean ground lamb

- ✓ 2 eggs, beaten
- ✓ 1 medium onion, chopped
- ✓ 2 tbsp. fresh cilantro, chopped
- ✓ 2 tbsp. fresh parsley leaves, chopped
- ✓ 1 tbsp. fresh mint leaves, chopped
- ✓ ½ tsp. red pepper flakes, crushed
- ✓ ¼ tsp. cayenne powder
- ✓ ¼ tsp. garlic powder
- ✓ Salt and ground black pepper, as required
- ✓ 3 tbsp. olive oil
- ✓ 8 C. fresh baby spinach

1. In a large-sized bowl, add all ingredients except for oil and mix until well blended.
2. Make desired-sized balls from mixture.
3. In an oven-safe pan that will fit in the Breville Smart Oven Air Fryer Pro, heat oil over medium heat and cook the meatballs for 4-5 minutes or until golden brown from all sides.
4. Remove the pan of meatballs from heat and cover the pan with a lid.
5. Arrange the pan over the wire rack.
6. Select "SLOW COOK" of Breville Smart Oven Air Fryer Pro and set on "Low".
7. Adjust the time for 7 hours and press "Start/Stop" to begin cooking.
8. After cooking time is finished, remove the pan from oven.
9. Remove the lid of pan and serve hot alongside the spinach.

Per Serving:
Calories: 285| Fat: 14.8g| Carbs: 2.7g|
Fiber: 1.1g| Protein: 34.3g

SEASONED PORK LOIN

Prep Time: 10 mins.| Cook Time: 30 mins.| Serves: 6

✓ 2 lb. pork loin
✓ 2 tbsp. olive oil, divided
✓ 2-3 tbsp. barbecue seasoning rub

1. Arrange a wire rack in a baking dish.
2. Coat the pork loin with oil evenly and then rub with barbecue seasoning rub generously.
3. Arrange the pork loin into the prepared baking dish.
4. Select "BAKE" of Breville Smart Oven Air Fryer Pro and adjust the temperature to 350 °F.
5. Adjust the time for 30 minutes and press "Start/Stop" to begin preheating.
6. As the unit beeps to show that it is preheated, arrange the baking dish over the wire rack.
7. After cooking time is finished, remove the baking dish from oven and place the pork loin onto a cutting board.
8. With a piece of foil, wrap the pork loin for about 10 minutes before slicing.
9. Cut the pork loin into desired-sized slices and serve.

Per Serving:
Calories: 421 | Fat: 25.7g | Carbs: 2g | Fiber: 0g | Protein: 41.3g

HERBED PORK CHOPS
Prep Time: 15 mins. | Cook Time: 12 mins. | Serves: 4

✓ 2 garlic cloves, minced
✓ ½ tbsp. fresh rosemary, chopped
✓ ½ tbsp. fresh parsley, chopped
✓ 2 tbsp. olive oil
✓ ¾ tbsp. Dijon mustard
✓ 1 tbsp. ground cumin
✓ 1 tsp. white sugar
✓ Salt and ground black pepper, as required
✓ 4 (6-oz.) (1-inch thick) pork chops

1. In a bowl, blend together the garlic, herbs, oil, mustard, cumin, sugar, and salt.
2. Add pork chops and coat with marinade generously.
3. Cover the bowl and refrigerate for about 2-3 hours.
4. Remove the chops from the refrigerator and set aside at room temperature for about 30 minutes.
5. Arrange the chops into the greased baking pan.
6. Select "AIRFRY/SUPER CONVECTION" of Breville Smart Oven Air Fryer Pro and then adjust the temperature to 390 °F.
7. Adjust the time for 12 minutes and press "Start/Stop" to begin preheating.
8. As the unit beeps to show that it is preheated, place the baking pan over the rack.
9. Flip the chops once halfway through.
10. After cooking time is finished, remove the baking pan from oven.
11. Serve hot.

Per Serving:
Calories: 342 | Fat: 28.3g | Carbs: 1.1g | Fiber: 0.3g | Protein: 19.4g

PORK WITH MUSHROOMS

Prep Time: 15 mins. | Cook Time: 4 hrs. | Serves: 5

- ✓ 1 yellow onion, sliced
- ✓ 1½ lb. pork tenderloin, cut into slices
- ✓ ½ lb. fresh button mushrooms, sliced
- ✓ 2 tbsp. olive oil
- ✓ Salt and ground black pepper, as required
- ✓ 2 C. chicken broth

1. Lightly grease a Dutch oven that will fit in the Breville Smart Oven Air Fryer Pro.
2. In the bottom of pot, arrange the onion slices and top with the pork tenderloin, followed by the mushroom slices.
3. Sprinkle with salt and black pepper and pour the broth on top.
4. Arrange the Dutch oven over the wire rack.
5. Select "SLOW COOK" of Breville Smart Oven Air Fryer Pro and set on "High".
6. Adjust the time for 4 hours and press "Start/Stop" to begin cooking.
7. After cooking time is finished, remove the Dutch oven from oven.
8. Open the lid and stir the mixture.
9. Serve hot.

Per Serving:
Calories: 276 | Fat: 11.1g | Carbs: 3.9g | Fiber: 0.9g | Protein: 39.2g

PORK MEATLOAF

Prep Time: 15 mins. | Cook Time: 1 hr. 5 mins. | Serves: 8

For Meatloaf:
- ✓ 2 lb. lean ground turkey
- ✓ 1 C. quick-cooking oats

- ✓ ½ C. carrot, peeled and shredded
- ✓ 1 medium onion, chopped
- ✓ ½ C. whole milk
- ✓ ¼ of egg, beaten
- ✓ 2 tbsp. ketchup
- ✓ 1 tsp. garlic powder
- ✓ ¼ tsp. ground black pepper

For Topping:
- ✓ ¼ C. ketchup
- ✓ ¼ C. quick-cooking oats

1. For meatloaf: in a large-sized bowl, add all ingredients and mix until well blended.
2. For topping: in a separate bowl, add all ingredients and mix until well blended.
3. Transfer the mixture into a greased loaf pan and top with the topping mixture.
4. Select "BAKE" of Breville Smart Oven Air Fryer Pro and adjust the temperature to 350 °F.
5. Adjust the time for 65 minutes and press "Start/Stop" to begin preheating.
6. As the unit beeps to show that it is preheated, arrange the loaf pan over the wire rack.
7. After cooking time is finished, remove the loaf pan from oven and place the loaf pan onto a wire rack for about 10 minutes before slicing.
8. Then invert the meatloaf onto the wire rack.
9. Cut into desired-sized slices and serve.

Per Serving:
Calories: 239 | Fat: 9.1g | Carbs: 14.5g | Fiber: 1.8g | Protein: 25.1g

PORK STUFFED BELL PEPPERS

Prep Time: 20 mins. | Cook Time: 1 hr 10 mins. | Serves: 4

- ✓ 4 medium green bell peppers
- ✓ 2/3-lb. ground pork
- ✓ 2 C. cooked white rice
- ✓ 1½ C. marinara sauce, divided

- ✓ 1 tsp. Worcestershire sauce
- ✓ 1 tsp. Italian seasoning
- ✓ Salt and ground black pepper, as required
- ✓ ½ C. mozzarella cheese, shredded

1. Remove the top of each bell pepper and then discard the seeds.
2. Heat a large-sized wok over medium heat and cook the pork for bout 6-8 minutes, breaking into crumbles.
3. Add rice, ¾ C. of marinara sauce, Worcestershire sauce, Italian seasoning, salt and black pepper and stir to combine.
4. Remove the wok of rice mixture from heat.
5. Arrange the stuffed bell peppers into the greased baking dish.
6. Carefully stuff each bell pepper with the pork mixture and top each with the remaining sauce.
7. Select "BAKE" of Breville Smart Oven Air Fryer Pro and adjust the temperature to 350 °F.
8. Adjust the time for 60 minutes and press "Start/Stop" to begin preheating.
9. As the unit beeps to show that it is preheated, arrange the baking dish over the wire rack.
10. After 50 minutes of cooking, top each bell pepper with cheese.
11. After cooking time is finished, remove the baking dish from oven.
12. Serve warm.

Per Serving:
Calories: 293 | Fat: 18.2g | Carbs: 15.6g | Fiber: 2.9g | Protein: 18.6g

FISH & SEAFOOD RECIPES

BUTTERED SALMON
Prep Time: 5 mins.| Cook Time: 10 mins.| Serves: 2

- ✓ Non-stick cooking spray
- ✓ 2 (6-oz.) salmon fillets
- ✓ Salt and ground black pepper, as required
- ✓ 1 tbsp. unsalted butter, melted

1. Grease the air fryer basket of Breville Smart Oven Air Fryer Pro with cooking spray.
2. Season each salmon fillet with salt and black pepper and then coat with the butter.
3. Arrange the salmon fillets into the prepared air fryer basket.
4. Select "AIRFRY/SUPER CONVECTION" of Breville Smart Oven Air Fryer Pro and then adjust the temperature to 360 °F.
5. Adjust the time for 10 minutes and press "Start/Stop" to begin preheating.
6. As the unit beeps to show that it is preheated, insert the air fryer basket in the oven.
7. After cooking time is finished, remove the air fryer basket from oven and transfer the salmon fillets onto serving plates.
8. Serve hot.

Per Serving:
Calories: 276| Fat: 16.3g| Carbs: 0g| Fiber: 0| Protein: 33.1g

SPICY SALMON
Prep Time: 10 mins.| Cook Time: 11mins.| Serves: 2

- ✓ 1 tsp. smoked paprika
- ✓ 1 tsp. cayenne powder
- ✓ 1 tsp. onion powder
- ✓ 1 tsp. garlic powder
- ✓ Salt and ground black pepper, as required
- ✓ 2 (6-oz.) (1½-inch thick) salmon fillets
- ✓ 2 tsp. olive oil

1. In a bowl, add spices and mix well.
2. Drizzle the salmon fillets with oil and then rub with the spice mixture.
3. Arrange the salmon fillets into the prepared air fryer basket, skin-side up.
4. Select "AIRFRY/SUPER CONVECTION" of Breville Smart Oven Air Fryer Pro and then adjust the temperature to 390 °F.
5. Adjust the time for 11 minutes and press "Start/Stop" to begin preheating.
6. As the unit beeps to show that it is preheated, insert the air fryer basket in the oven.
7. After cooking time is finished, remove the air fryer basket from oven and

transfer the salmon fillets onto serving plates.

8. Serve hot.

Per Serving:
Calories: 280 | Fat: 2.2g | Carbs: 3.1g | Fiber: 0.8g | Protein: 33.6g

CRUSTED SALMON

Prep Time: 10 mins. | Cook Time: 15 mins. | Serves: 2

- ✓ 2 (6-oz.) skinless salmon fillets
- ✓ Salt and ground black pepper, as required
- ✓ 3 tbsp. walnuts, chopped finely
- ✓ 3 tbsp. quick-cooking oats, crushed
- ✓ 2 tbsp. olive oil

1. Grease the enamel roasting pan of Breville Smart Oven Air Fryer Pro with cooking spray. Set aside.
2. Rub each salmon fillet with salt and black pepper evenly.
3. In a bowl, blend together the walnuts, oats and oil.
4. Arrange the salmon fillets into the roasting pan in a single layer.
5. Place the oat mixture over each salmon fillet and then gently press down.
6. Select "BAKE" of oven and adjust the temperature to 400 °F.
7. Adjust the time for 15 minutes and press "Start/Stop" to begin preheating.
8. As the unit beeps to show that it is preheated, insert the roasting pan in the oven.
9. After cooking time is finished, remove the baking pan from oven and transfer the salmon fillets onto serving plates.
10. Serve hot.

Per Serving:
Calories: 446 | Fat: 31.9g | Carbs: 6.4g | Fiber: 1.6g | Protein: 36.8g

RANCH TILAPIA

Prep Time: 10 mins. | Cook Time: 13 mins. | Serves: 4

- ✓ ¾ C. cornflakes, crushed
- ✓ (1-oz.) packet dry ranch-style dressing mix
- ✓ 2½ tbsp. vegetable oil
- ✓ 2 eggs
- ✓ 4 (6-oz.) tilapia fillets

1. In a shallow bowl, beat the eggs.
2. In a separate bowl, add cornflakes, ranch dressing, and oil and mix until a crumbly mixture forms.
3. Dip the fish fillets into egg and then coat with the breadcrumbs mixture.
4. Arrange the tilapia fillets into the prepared air fryer basket.
5. Select "AIRFRY/SUPER CONVECTION" of Breville Smart Oven Air Fryer Pro and then adjust the temperature to 356 °F.
6. Adjust the time for 13 minutes and press "Start/Stop" to begin preheating.
7. As the unit beeps to show that it is preheated, insert the air fryer basket in the oven.
8. After cooking time is finished, remove the remove tilapia fillets from oven and transfer onto serving plates.
9. Serve hot.

Per Serving:
Calories: 267 | Fat: 12.2g | Carbs: 5.1g | Fiber: 0.2g | Protein: 34.9g

GLAZED HALIBUT
Prep Time: 10 mins. | Cook Time: 15 mins. | Serves: 3

- ✓ 1 garlic clove, minced
- ✓ ¼ tsp. fresh ginger, finely grated
- ✓ ½ C. cooking wine
- ✓ ½ C. low-sodium soy sauce
- ✓ ¼ C. fresh orange juice
- ✓ 2 tbsp. fresh lime juice
- ✓ ¼ C. white sugar
- ✓ ¼ tsp. red pepper flakes, crushed
- ✓ 1 lb. halibut steak

1. In a medium-sized saucepan, add garlic, ginger, wine, soy sauce, juices, sugar, and red pepper flakes and bring to a boil.
2. Cook for about 3-4 minutes, stirring continuously.
3. Remove the pan of marinade from heat and let it cool.
4. In a small-sized bowl, add half of the marinade and reserve in a refrigerator.
5. In a resealable bag, add remaining marinade and halibut steak.
6. Seal the bag and shake to coat well.
7. Refrigerate for about 30 minutes.
8. Grease the air fryer basket of Breville Smart Oven Air Fryer Pro with cooking spray.
9. Place the halibut steak into the prepared air fryer basket.
10. Select "AIRFRY/SUPER CONVECTION" of oven and then adjust the temperature to 390 °F.
11. Adjust the time for 11 minutes and press "Start/Stop" to begin preheating.
12. As the unit beeps to show that it is preheated, insert the air fryer basket in the oven.
13. After cooking time is finished, remove the remove halibut steak from oven and place onto a platter.
14. Cut the steak into 3 equal-sized pieces and coat with the remaining glaze.
15. Serve immediately.

Per Serving:
Calories: 218 | Fat: 1.1g | Carbs: 17.4g | Fiber: 0.1 Protein: 29.7g

CRISPY COD
Prep Time: 15 mins. | Cook Time: 15 mins. | Serves: 4

- ✓ 4 (4-oz.) (¾-inch thick) cod fillets
- ✓ Salt, as required
- ✓ 2 tbsp. all-purpose flour
- ✓ 2 eggs
- ✓ ½ C. panko breadcrumbs
- ✓ 1 tsp. fresh dill, minced
- ✓ ½ tsp. dry mustard
- ✓ ½ tsp. lemon zest, grated
- ✓ ½ tsp. onion powder
- ✓ ½ tsp. paprika
- ✓ Non-stick cooking spray

1. Season each cod fillet with salt generously.
2. In a shallow dish, place the flour.
3. Crack both eggs in a second shallow dish and whisk well.
4. In a third shallow dish, blend together the panko, dill, lemon zest, mustard and spices.
5. Coat each cod fillet with the flour, then dip into beaten eggs and finally, coat with panko mixture.
6. Arrange the cod fillets into the air fryer basket and spray the tops with cooking spray.
7. Select "AIRFRY/SUPER CONVECTION" of Breville Smart

Oven Air Fryer Pro and then adjust the temperature to 400 °F.

8. Adjust the time for 15 minutes and press "Start/Stop" to begin preheating.\As the unit beeps to show that it is preheated, insert the air fryer basket in the oven.
9. Flip the cod fillets once halfway through.
10. After cooking time is finished, remove the air fryer basket from oven and transfer the cod fillets onto serving plates.
11. Serve hot.

Per Serving:
Calories: 99 | Fat: 4.3g | Carbs: 5.9g | Fiber: 0.4g | Protein: 24g

VINEGAR SEA BASS
Prep Time: 10 mins. | Cook Time: 12 mins. | Serves: 2

- ✓ 2 (5-oz.) sea bass fillets
- ✓ 1 garlic clove, minced
- ✓ 1 tsp. fresh dill, minced
- ✓ 1 tbsp. olive oil
- ✓ 1 tbsp. balsamic vinegar
- ✓ Salt and ground black pepper, as required

1. In a large-sized resealable bag, add all ingredients.
2. Seal the bag and shale well to mix.
3. Refrigerate to marinate for at least 30-40 minutes.
4. Remove the fish fillets from bag and shake off the excess marinade.
5. Arrange the fish fillets into the greased enamel roasting pan in a single layer.
6. Select "BAKE" of Breville Smart Oven Air Fryer Pro and adjust the temperature to 450 °F.
7. Adjust the time for 12 minutes and press "Start/Stop" to begin preheating.

8. As the unit beeps to show that it is preheated, insert the roasting pan in the oven.
9. Flip the fish fillets once halfway through.
10. After cooking time is finished, remove the roasting pan from oven and transfer the fish fillets onto serving plates.
11. Serve hot.

Per Serving:
Calories: 241 | Fat: 10.7g | Carbs: 0.9g | Fiber: 0.1g | Protein: 33.7g

HADDOCK WITH BELL PEPPERS
Prep Time: 15 mins. | Cook Time: 4 hrs. | Serves: 4

- ✓ 1 (15-oz.) can diced tomatoes
- ✓ 1green bell pepper, seeded and chopped
- ✓ 1 small onion, diced
- ✓ 1 garlic cloves, minced
- ✓ 1 lb. haddock fillets
- ✓ ¼ tsp. dried thyme
- ✓ ¼ tsp. dried oregano
- ✓ ¼ tsp. dried rosemary
- ✓ Salt and ground black pepper, as required
- ✓ 1/3 C. chicken broth

1. Lightly grease a Dutch oven that will fit in the Breville Smart Oven Air Fryer Pro.
2. In the greased pot, place the tomatoes, bell pepper, onion and garlic and stir to combine.
3. Place the fish fillets on top of the tomato mixture and sprinkle with herbs, salt and black pepper.
4. Place the broth on top evenly.
5. Arrange the Dutch oven over the wire rack.
6. Select "SLOW COOK" of Breville Smart Oven Air Fryer Pro and set on "High".
7. Adjust the time for 4 hours and press "Start/Stop" to begin cooking.

8. After cooking time is finished, remove the Dutch oven from oven.
9. Remove the lid of pan and serve hot.

Per Serving:
Calories: 166 | Fat: 3.1g | Carbs: 8.5g | Fiber: 2.2g | Protein: 25.8g

PRAWNS IN BUTTER SAUCE
Prep Time: 15 mins. | Cook Time: 6 mins. | Serves: 2

- ½ lb. large prawns, peeled and deveined
- 1 large garlic clove, minced
- 1 tbsp. unsalted butter, melted
- 1 tsp. fresh lemon zest, grated

1. In a large-sized bowl, add all ingredients and toss to coat well.
2. Set the bowl of prawns aside at room temperature for about 30 minutes.
3. Arrange the prawn mixture into a baking dish.
4. Select "BAKE" of Breville Smart Oven Air Fryer Pro and adjust the temperature to 450 °F.
5. Adjust the time for 6 minutes and press "Start/Stop" to begin preheating.
6. As the unit beeps to show that it is preheated, arrange the baking dish over the wire rack.
7. After cooking time is finished, remove the baking dish from oven and transfer the shrimp onto serving plates.
8. Serve immediately.

Per Serving:
Calories: 189 | Fat: 7.7g | Carbs: 2.4g | Fiber: 0.1g | Protein: 26g

SHRIMP WITH TOMATOES
Prep Time: 15 mins. | Cook Time: 7¼ hrs. | Serves: 4

- 1 (14-oz.) can peeled tomatoes, chopped finely
- 4 oz. canned tomato paste
- 2 garlic cloves, minced
- 2 tbsp. fresh parsley, chopped
- Salt and ground black pepper, as required
- 1 tsp. lemon pepper
- 2 lb. cooked shrimp, peeled and deveined

1. In an oven-safe pan that will fit in the Breville Smart Oven Air Fryer Pro, place all ingredients except for shrimp and stir to combine.
2. Cover the pan with a lid.
3. Arrange the pan over the wire rack.
4. Select "SLOW COOK" of Breville Smart Oven Air Fryer Pro and set on "Low".
5. Adjust the time for 7 hours and press "Start/Stop" to begin cooking.
6. After cooking time is finished, remove the pan from oven.
7. Remove the lid of pan and stir in the shrimp.
8. Again, arrange the pan over the wire rack.

9. Select "SLOW COOK" of Breville Smart Oven Air Fryer Pro and set on "High".
10. Adjust the time for 15 minutes and press "Start/Stop" to begin cooking
11. After cooking time is finished, remove the pan from oven.
12. Remove the lid of pan and stir well.
13. Serve hot.

Per Serving:
Calories: 315 | Fat: 4.2g | Carbs: 13.6g | Fiber: 2.6g | Protein: 54g

SHRIMP SCAMPI

Prep Time: 10 mins. | Cook Time: 7 mins. | Serves: 3

- ✓ 4 tbsp. unsalted butter
- ✓ 1 tbsp. fresh lemon juice
- ✓ 1 tbsp. garlic, minced
- ✓ 2 tsp. red pepper flakes, crushed
- ✓ 1 lb. shrimp, peeled and deveined
- ✓ 2 tbsp. fresh basil, chopped
- ✓ 1 tbsp. fresh chives, chopped
- ✓ 2 tbsp. dry white wine

1. Arrange a 7-inch round baking dish in the air fryer basket.
2. Insert the basket in Breville Smart Oven Air Fryer Pro.
3. Select "AIRFRY/SUPER CONVECTION" of Breville Smart Oven Air Fryer Pro and then adjust the temperature to 325 °F.
4. Adjust the time for 7 minutes and press "Start/Stop" to begin preheating.
5. As the unit beeps to show that it is preheated, carefully remove the hot pan from Air fryer basket.
6. In the heated pan, place butter, lemon juice, garlic, and red pepper flakes and stir to combine.
7. Return the pan into air fryer basket and insert in the oven.
8. After 1 minute of cooking, stir the mixture once.

9. After 2 minutes of cooking, stir in the shrimp, basil, chives and wine.
10. While cooking, stir the mixture once after 5 minutes.
11. After cooking time is finished, remove the air fryer basket from oven and place the pan onto a wire rack for about 1 minute.
12. Stir the mixture and transfer onto serving plates.
13. Serve hot.

Per Serving:
Calories: 245 | Fat: 15.7g | Carbs: 3.1g | Fiber: 0.3g | Protein: 26.4g

SCALLOPS WITH CAPERS SAUCE

Prep Time: 15 mins. | Cook Time: 6 mins. | Serves: 2

- ✓ 8 (1-oz.) sea scallops, cleaned and patted dry
- ✓ Salt and ground black pepper, as required
- ✓ 2 tbsp. olive oil
- ✓ 2 tbsp. fresh parsley leaves, finely chopped
- ✓ 2 tsp. capers, finely chopped
- ✓ 1 tsp. fresh lemon zest, finely grated
- ✓ ½ tsp. garlic, finely chopped

1. Sprinkle each scallop evenly with salt and black pepper.
2. Arrange scallops into the prepared air fryer basket in a single layer.
3. Select "AIRFRY/SUPER CONVECTION" of Breville Smart Oven Air Fryer Pro and then adjust the temperature to 400 °F.
4. Adjust the time for 6 minutes and press "Start/Stop" to begin preheating.
5. As the unit beeps to show that it is preheated, insert the air fryer basket in the oven.
6. Meanwhile, for sauce: in a medium-sized bowl, add remaining ingredients and mix well.

7. After cooking time is finished, remove the air fryer basket from oven and transfer the scallops onto serving plates.
8. Top with the sauce and serve immediately.

Per Serving:
Calories: 224 | Fat: 14.9g | Carbs: 3.5g | Fiber: 0.3g | Protein: 19.3g

CRAB CAKES
Prep Time: 15 mins. | Cook Time: 10 mins. | Serves: 4

- ¼ C. bell pepper, seeded and chopped finely
- 2 scallions, chopped finely
- 2 tbsp. mayonnaise
- 2 tbsp. breadcrumbs
- 1 tbsp. Dijon mustard
- 1 tsp. old bay seasoning
- 8 oz. lump crabmeat, drained
- 4 cups fresh baby kale

1. Grease the enamel roasting pan of Breville Smart Oven Air Fryer Pro with cooking spray. Set aside.
1. In a large-sized bowl, add all ingredients except crabmeat and mix until well blended.
2. Gently fold in the crabmeat.
3. Make 4 equal-sized patties from the mixture.
4. Arrange the patties onto the prepared roasting pan.

5. Select "AIRFRY/SUPER CONVECTION" of Breville Smart Oven Air Fryer Pro and then adjust the temperature to 370 °F
6. Adjust the time for 10 minutes and press "Start/Stop" to begin preheating.
7. As the unit beeps to show that it is preheated, insert the roasting pan in the oven.
8. After cooking time is finished, remove the roasting pan from oven and transfer the crab cakes onto serving plates.
9. Serve hot alongside the kale.

Per Serving:
Calories: 124 | Fat: 7.4g | Carbs: 13.4g | Fiber: 1.6g | Protein: 11.1g

CREAMY MUSSELS
Prep Time: 20 mins. | Cook Time: 2 hrs. 20 mins. | Serves: 6

- 1 C. chicken broth
- 1 tbsp. red boat fish sauce
- 1 small yellow onion, chopped
- 2 garlic cloves, grated
- 1 lemongrass stalk, smashed
- 1 small Serrano pepper, chopped
- 2 lb. fresh mussels, scrubbed and debearded
- 1½ C. unsweetened coconut milk
- ¼ C. fresh cilantro leaves
- 1 tsp. fresh lime zest, grated
- 1 tbsp. fresh lime juice

1. In an oven-safe pan that will fit in the Breville Smart Oven Air Fryer Pro, add broth, fish sauce, onion, garlic, lemongrass and Serrano pepper and stir to combine.
2. Cover the pan with a lid.
3. Arrange the pan over the wire rack.
4. Select "SLOW COOK" of Breville Smart Oven Air Fryer Pro and set on "High".
5. Adjust the time for 2 hours and 20 minutes and press "Start/Stop" to begin cooking.

6. After cooking time is finished, remove the pan from oven.
7. After 2 hours of cooking, stir in the mussels and coconut milk.
8. Remove the lid of pan and stir in the cilantro, lime zest and juice.
9. Serve hot.

Per Serving:
Calories: 284 | Fat: 17.9g | Carbs: 10.6g | Fiber: 1.7g | Protein: 21.1g

SALMON & SHRIMP STEW

Prep Time: 15 mins. | Cook Time: 4 hrs. | Serves: 8

- ✓ 2 tbsp. olive oil
- ✓ 1 lb. tomatoes, chopped
- ✓ 1 large yellow onion, chopped finely
- ✓ 2 garlic cloves, minced
- ✓ 2 tsp. curry powder
- ✓ 6 sprigs fresh parsley
- ✓ Salt and ground black pepper, as required
- ✓ 1½ C. chicken broth
- ✓ 1½ lb. salmon, cut into cubes
- ✓ 1½ lb. shrimp, peeled and deveined

1. In an oven-safe pan that will fit in the Breville Smart Oven Air Fryer Pro, place all ingredients except for seafood and stir to combine.
2. Cover the pan with a lid.
3. Arrange the pan over the wire rack.
4. Select "SLOW COOK" of Breville Smart Oven Air Fryer Pro and set on "High".
5. Adjust the time for 4 hours and press "Start/Stop" to begin cooking.
6. After cooking time is finished, remove the pan from oven.
7. Remove the lid of pan and stir in the seafood.
8. Cover the pan with a lid.
9. Again, arrange the pan over the wire rack.
10. Select "SLOW COOK" of Breville Smart Oven Air Fryer Pro and set on "Low".
11. Adjust the time for 50 minutes and press "Start/Stop" to begin cooking.
12. After cooking time is finished, remove the pan from oven.
13. Remove the lid of pan and stir the mixture well.
14. Serve hot.

Per Serving:
Calories: 272 | Fat: 10.7g | Carbs: 6g | Fiber: 1.3g | Protein: 37.6g

VEGETARAIN RECIPES

STUFFED TOMATOES

Prep Time: 15 mins.| Cook Time: 15 mins.| Serves: 2

- ✓ 2 large tomatoes
- ✓ ½ C. broccoli, finely chopped
- ✓ ½ C. cheddar cheese, shredded
- ✓ 1 tbsp. unsalted butter, melted
- ✓ ½ tsp. dried thyme, crushed

1. Slice the top of each tomato and scoop out pulp and seeds.
2. In a bowl, blend together the chopped broccoli and cheese.
3. Stuff each tomato evenly with broccoli mixture.
4. Arrange tomatoes into the prepared air fryer basket and drizzle with butter.
5. Select "AIRFRY/SUPER CONVECTION" of Breville Smart Oven Air Fryer Pro and then adjust the temperature to 355 °F.
6. Adjust the time for 15 minutes and press "Start/Stop" to begin preheating.
7. As the unit beeps to show that it is preheated, insert the air fryer basket in the oven.
8. After cooking time is finished, remove the air fryer basket from oven and transfer the tomatoes onto a serving platter.
9. Set aside to cool slightly.
10. Garnish with thyme and serve.

Per Serving:
Calories: 206| Fat: 15.6g| Carbs: 9.1g| Fiber: 2.9g| Protein: 9.4g

STUFFED ZUCCHINI

Prep Time: 15 mins.| Cook Time: 35 mins.| Serves: 4

- ✓ 2 zucchinis, cut in half lengthwise
- ✓ ½ tsp. garlic powder
- ✓ Salt, as required
- ✓ 1 tsp. olive oil
- ✓ 4 oz. fresh mushrooms, chopped
- ✓ 4 oz. carrots, peeled and shredded
- ✓ 3 oz. onion, chopped
- ✓ 4 oz. goat cheese, crumbled
- ✓ 12 fresh basil leaves
- ✓ ½ tsp. onion powder

1. Grease a baking dish with cooking spray. Set aside.
2. Carefully scoop the flesh from the middle of each zucchini half.
3. Sprinkle each zucchini half with a little garlic powder and salt.
4. Then arrange the zucchini halves into the greased baking dish.
5. Select "BAKE" of Breville Smart Oven Air Fryer Pro and adjust the temperature to 450 °F.
6. Adjust the time for 20 minutes and press "Start/Stop" to begin preheating.

7. As the unit beeps to show that it is preheated, arrange the baking dish over the wire rack.
8. Meanwhile, in a non-stick wok, heat oil over medium heat and cook the mushrooms, carrots, onion, onion powder and salt and cook for about 5-6 minutes
9. After cooking time is finished, remove the baking dish from oven and set aside.
10. Stuff each zucchini half with veggie mixture and top with basil leaves, followed by the cheese.
11. Select "BAKE" of Breville Smart Oven Air Fryer Pro and adjust the temperature to 450 °F
12. Adjust the time for 15 minutes and press "Start/Stop" to begin preheating
13. As the unit beeps to show that it is preheated, arrange the baking dish over the wire rack.
14. After cooking time is finished, remove the baking dish from oven and transfer the zucchini halves onto serving plates.
15. Serve warm.

Per Serving:
Calories: 181 | Fat: 11.6g | Carbs: 10.1g | Fiber: 2.6g | Protein: 11.3g

POTATO GRATIN
Prep Time: 10 mins. | Cook Time: 25 mins. | Serves: 4

- ✓ 2 large potatoes, sliced thinly
- ✓ 5½ tbsp. light cream
- ✓ 2 eggs

- ✓ 1 tbsp. plain flour
- ✓ ½ C. cheddar cheese, grated

1. Arrange the potato slices into the air fryer basket.
2. Select "AIRFRY/SUPER CONVECTION" of Breville Smart Oven Air Fryer Pro and then adjust the temperature to 355 °F.
3. Adjust the time for 10 minutes and press "Start/Stop" to begin preheating.
4. As the unit beeps to show that it is preheated, insert the air fryer basket in the oven.
5. Meanwhile, in a bowl, add cream, eggs and flour and mix until a thick sauce forms.
6. After cooking time is finished, remove the air fryer basket from oven.
7. Divide the potato slices in 4 ramekins evenly and top with the egg mixture evenly, followed by the cheese.
8. Arrange the ramekins of potato mixture into the air fryer basket and insert in the oven.
9. Select "AIRFRY/SUPER CONVECTION" of Breville Smart Oven Air Fryer Pro and then adjust the temperature to 390 °F.
10. Adjust the time for 10 minutes and press "Start/Stop" to begin cooking.
11. After cooking time is finished, remove the air fryer basket from oven and place the ramekins onto a wire rack to cool slightly.
12. Serve warm.

Per Serving:
Calories: 233 | Fat: 8g | Carbs: 31.3g | Fiber: 4.5g | Protein: 9.7g

BUTTERED VEGGIES
Prep Time: 15 mins. | Cook Time: 20 mins. | Serves: 3

- ✓ Non-stick cooking spray
- ✓ 1 C. potato, chopped

- ✓ 1 C. beet, peeled and chopped
- ✓ 1 C. carrot, peeled and chopped
- ✓ 2 garlic cloves, minced
- ✓ Salt and ground black pepper, as required
- ✓ 3 tbsp. olive oil

1. Grease the enamel roasting pan of Breville Smart Oven Air Fryer Pro with cooking spray. Set aside.
2. In a large-sized bowl, place all ingredients and toss to coat well.
3. Place the veggie mixture into the greased roasting pan.
4. Select "BAKE" of oven and adjust the temperature to 450 °F.
5. Adjust the time for 20 minutes and press "Start/Stop" to begin preheating.
6. As the unit beeps to show that it is preheated, insert the roasting pan in the oven.
7. Toss the veggie mixture once halfway through.
8. After cooking time is finished, remove the roasting pan from oven and transfer the vegetable mixture onto serving plates.
9. Serve hot.

Per Serving:
Calories: 197| Fat: 14.2g| Carbs: 17.8g| Fiber: 3.3g| Protein: 2.2g

SEASONED VEGGIES
Prep Time: 15 mins.| Cook Time: 12 mins.| Serves: 3

- ✓ Non-stick cooking spray
- ✓ ½ lb. baby carrots
- ✓ 1 C. broccoli florets
- ✓ 1 C. cauliflower florets
- ✓ 1 tbsp. olive oil
- ✓ 1 tbsp. Italian seasoning
- ✓ Salt and ground black pepper, as required

1. Grease the air fryer basket of Breville Smart Oven Air Fryer Pro with cooking spray.
2. In a bowl, add all ingredients and toss to coat well.
3. Place the vegetables in the prepared air fryer basket.
4. Select "AIRFRY/SUPER CONVECTION" of oven and then adjust the temperature to 380 °F.
5. Adjust the time for 18 minutes and press "Start/Stop" to begin preheating.
6. As the unit beeps to show that it is preheated, insert the air fryer basket in the oven.
7. After cooking time is finished, remove the air fryer basket from oven and transfer the vegetable mixture onto serving plates.
8. Serve hot.

Per Serving:
Calories: 88| Fat: 6.2g| Carbs: 7.9g| Fiber: 2.5g| Protein: 1.8g

VEGETARIAN LOAF
Prep Time: 20 mins.| Cook Time: 1½ hrs.| Serves: 6

- ✓ 1 (14½-oz.) can vegetable broth
- ✓ ¾ C. brown lentils, rinsed
- ✓ 1 tbsp. olive oil
- ✓ 1¾ C. carrots, peeled and shredded
- ✓ 1 C. fresh mushrooms, chopped
- ✓ 1 C. onion, chopped
- ✓ 1 tbsp. fresh parsley, minced
- ✓ 1 tbsp. fresh basil, minced

- ✓ ½ C. cooked brown rice
- ✓ 1 C. mozzarella cheese, shredded
- ✓ 1 large egg
- ✓ 1 large egg white
- ✓ Salt and ground black pepper, as required
- ✓ 2 tbsp. tomato paste
- ✓ 2 tbsp. water
- ✓ Non-stick cooking spray

1. In a pan, place the broth over medium-high heat and bring to a boil.
2. Stir in the lentils and again bring to a boil.
3. Adjust the heat to low and simmer, covered for about 30 minutes.
4. Remove the pan of broth from heat and set aside to cool slightly.
5. Meanwhile, in a large-sized wok, heat oil over medium heat and sauté the carrots, mushrooms and onion for about 10 minutes.
6. Stir in herbs and remove the wok of mushroom mixture from heat.
7. Transfer the veggie mixture into a large-sized bowl and set aside to cool slightly.
8. After cooling, add lentils, rice, cheese, egg, egg white and seasonings and lentils and mix until well blended.
9. In a small-sized bowl, stir together the tomato paste and water.
10. Line a loaf pan with parchment paper and then lightly grease it with cooking spray.
11. Place the mixture into the prepared loaf pan and top with water mixture.
12. Select "BAKE" of Breville Smart Oven Air Fryer Pro and adjust the temperature to 350 °F.
13. Adjust the time for 50 minutes and press "Start/Stop" to begin preheating.
14. As the unit beeps to show that it is preheated, arrange the loaf pan over the wire rack.
15. After cooking time is finished, remove the loaf pan from oven and place onto a wire rack for about 10 minutes before slicing.
16. Carefully invert the veggie loaf onto a platter.
17. Cut into desired-sized slices and serve.

Per Serving:
Calories: 229 | Fat: 5.1g | Carbs: 33.4g | Fiber: 9.4g | Protein: 12.8g

PITA BREAD PIZZA
Prep Time: 10 mins. | Cook Time: 50 mins. | Serves: 1

- ✓ 2 tbsp. marinara sauce
- ✓ 1 whole-wheat pita bread
- ✓ ½ C. fresh baby spinach leaves
- ✓ ½ of small plum tomato, cut into 4 slices
- ✓ ½ of garlic clove, sliced thinly
- ✓ ½ oz. part-skim mozzarella cheese, shredded
- ✓ ½ tbsp. Parmigiano-Reggiano cheese, shredded

1. Grease the air fryer basket of Breville Smart Oven Air Fryer Pro with cooking spray.
2. Arrange the pita bread onto a plate.
3. Spread marinara sauce over 1 side of each pita bread evenly.
4. Top with the spinach leaves, followed by tomato slices, garlic and cheeses.
5. Arrange the pita bread into the prepared air fryer basket.
6. Select "AIRFRY/SUPER CONVECTION" of oven and then adjust the temperature to 350 °F.
7. Adjust the time for 5 minutes and press "Start/Stop" to begin preheating.
8. As the unit beeps to show that it is preheated, insert the air fryer basket in the oven.
9. After cooking time is finished, remove the air fryer basket from oven and transfer the pizza onto a serving plate.
10. Set aside to cool slightly.
11. Serve warm.

Per Serving:
Calories: 262 | Fat: 5.8g | Carbs: 42.9g |
Fiber: 6.5g | Protein: 12.7g

TOFU IN SWEET & SOUR SAUCE
Prep Time: 20 mins. | Cook Time: 20 mins. | Serves: 4

For Tofu:
- ✓ 1 (14-oz.) block firm tofu, pressed, drained and cubed
- ✓ 1/3-½ C. arrowroot flour
- ✓ ½ tsp. sesame oil

For Sauce:
- ✓ 4 tbsp. low-sodium soy sauce
- ✓ 1½ tbsp. rice vinegar
- ✓ 1½ tbsp. chili sauce
- ✓ 1 tbsp. agave nectar
- ✓ 2 large garlic cloves, minced
- ✓ 1 tsp. fresh ginger, peeled and grated
- ✓ 2 scallions (green part), chopped

1. Grease the air fryer basket of Breville Smart Oven Air Fryer Pro with cooking spray.
2. In a bowl, blend together the tofu, arrowroot flour, and sesame oil.
3. Arrange the tofu cubes into the prepared air fryer basket.
4. Select "AIRFRY/SUPER CONVECTION" of oven and then adjust the temperature to 360 °F.
5. Adjust the time for 20 minutes and press "Start/Stop" to begin preheating.

6. As the unit beeps to show that it is preheated, insert the air fryer basket in the oven.
7. Flip the tofu cubes once halfway through.
8. Meanwhile, for sauce: in a medium-sized bowl, add all ingredients except for scallions and whisk until well blended.
9. After cooking time is finished, remove the air fryer basket from oven.
10. Transfer the tofu into a non-stick wok with sauce over medium heat and cook for about 3 minutes, stirring occasionally.
11. Garnish with scallions and serve hot.

Per Serving:
Calories: 115 | Fat: 4.8g | Carbs: 5.6g |
Fiber: 1.7g | Protein: 10.1g

TOFU WITH BROCCOLI
Prep Time: 15 mins. | Cook Time: 15 mins. | Serves: 3

- ✓ Non-stick cooking spray
- ✓ 8 oz. firm tofu, drained, pressed and cubed
- ✓ 1 head broccoli, cut into florets
- ✓ 1 tbsp. unsalted butter, melted
- ✓ tsp. ground turmeric
- ✓ ¼ tsp. paprika
- ✓ Salt and ground black pepper, as required

1. Grease a baking dish with cooking spray. Set aside.
2. In a large-sized bowl, add all ingredients and mix well.
3. Place the tofu mixture in the prepared baking dish
4. Select "AIRFRY/SUPER CONVECTION" of Breville Smart Oven Air Fryer Pro and then adjust the temperature to 390 °F.
5. Adjust the time for 15 minutes and press "Start/Stop" to begin preheating.

6. As the unit beeps to show that it is preheated, insert the baking dish in the oven.
7. Toss the tofu mixture once halfway through.
8. After cooking time is finished, remove the baking dish from oven and transfer the tofu mixture onto serving plates.
9. Serve hot.

Per Serving:
Calories: 119 | Fat: 7.4g | Carbs: 7.5g | Fiber: 3.1g | Protein: 8.7g

BROCCOLI SOUP
Prep Time: 15 mins. | Cook Time: 6 hrs. 10 mins. | Serves: 6

✓ 2 tbsp. unsalted butter
✓ 1 yellow onion, chopped
✓ 2 garlic cloves, minced
✓ 1 tbsp. fresh rosemary, chopped
✓ C. small broccoli florets
✓ 5 C. vegetable broth
✓ Salt and ground black pepper, as required
✓ 1 C. sour cream

1. In a Dutch oven that will fit in the Breville Smart Oven Air Fryer Pro, melt the butter over medium heat and sauté the onion and cook for about 3–4 minutes.
2. Add the garlic and rosemary and sauté for about 1 minute.

3. Stir in the broccoli, broth and black pepper and immediately remove from the heat.
9. . Cover the pan with a lid.
10. Arrange the pan over the wire rack.
11. Press "Slow Cooker" of Breville Smart Air Fryer Oven and set on "Low".
12. Adjust the timer of oven for 6 hours and press "Start/Stop" to begin cooking.
13. After cooking time is finished, remove the pan from oven.
14. Remove the lid of pan and stir in the sour cream.
15. With a stick blender, blend the soup until smooth.
16. Serve immediately.

Per Serving:
Calories: 179 | Fat: 13.3g | Carbs: 8.8g | Fiber: 2.2g | Protein: 7.3g

BEANS BURGERS
Prep Time: 15 mins. | Cook Time: 22 mins. | Serves: 4

✓ 1 C. cooked black beans
✓ 2 C. boiled potatoes, peeled and mashed
✓ 1 C. fresh spinach, chopped
✓ 1 C. fresh mushrooms, chopped
✓ 2 tsp. Chile lime seasoning
✓ Non-stick cooking spray
✓ 3 cups fresh baby arugula

1. In a large-sized bowl, add beans, potatoes, spinach, mushrooms, and seasoning and with your hands, mix until well blended.
2. Make 4 equal-sized patties from the mixture.
3. Spray the patties with cooking spray evenly.
4. Grease the air fryer basket of Breville Smart Oven Air Fryer Pro with cooking spray.
5. Arrange the patties into the prepared air fryer basket.

6. Select "AIRFRY/SUPER CONVECTION" of Breville Smart Oven Air Fryer Pro and then adjust the temperature to 370 °F.
7. Adjust the time for 22 minutes and press "Start/Stop" to begin preheating
8. As the unit beeps to show that it is preheated, insert the air fryer basket in the oven.
9. Flip the patties once after 12 minutes.
10. After cooking time is finished, remove the air fryer basket from oven.
11. Serve hot alongside the arugula.

Per Serving:
Calories: 118| Fat: 0.4g| Carbs: 25.1g| Fiber: 7.2g| Protein: 6.5g

BEANS & QUINOA CHILI
Prep Time: 15 mins.| Cook Time: 6 hrs. 10 mins.| Serves: 6

- ✓ 2 tsp. olive oil
- ✓ 1 large yellow onion, chopped
- ✓ 2 celery stalks, chopped
- ✓ 3 garlic cloves, chopped
- ✓ ¼ C. water
- ✓ 2 tbsp. tomato paste
- ✓ 1 jalapeño pepper, chopped finely
- ✓ 2 tsp. red chili powder
- ✓ 1 tsp. ground coriander
- ✓ 1 tsp. ground cumin
- ✓ ½ tsp. ground cinnamon
- ✓ ½ tsp. smoked paprika
- ✓ Pinch of cayenne powder
- ✓ 3 C. vegetable broth
- ✓ 3 C. cooked black beans
- ✓ 1 C. uncooked quinoa, rinsed
- ✓ 1-1¼ lb. butternut squash, peeled and cubed
- ✓ 1 (15-oz.) can fire-roasted tomatoes with juice
- ✓ 1 small avocado, peeled, pitted and sliced

1. In an oven-safe pan that will fit in the Breville Smart Oven Air Fryer Pro, heat oil over medium heat and cook the onion and celery for about 5-7 minutes, stirring frequently.
2. Add garlic and sauté for about 1 minute.
3. Add water, tomato paste, chipotle and spices and cook for about 1 minute, stirring continuously.
4. Remove the pan of onion mixture from heat and stir in the broth, black beans, quinoa, squash and tomatoes with juice.
5. Cover the pan with a lid.
6. Arrange the pan over the wire rack.
7. Select "SLOW COOK" of Breville Smart Oven Air Fryer Pro and set on "Low".
8. Adjust the time for 6 hours and press "Start/Stop" to begin cooking.
9. After cooking time is finished, remove the pan from oven
10. Remove the lid of pan and stir the mixture well.
11. Serve hot with the garnishing of avocado slices.

Per Serving:
Calories: 397| Fat: 11.5g| Carbs: 60.6g| Fiber: 15.8g| Protein: 17.1g

VEGGIE RICE
Prep Time: 15 mins.| Cook Time: 18 mins.| Serves: 4

- ✓ Non-stick cooking spray
- ✓ 2 C. cooked white rice
- ✓ 1 tbsp. vegetable oil
- ✓ 2 tsp. sesame oil, toasted and divided

- ✓ 1 tbsp. water
- ✓ Salt and ground white pepper, as required
- ✓ 1 large egg, lightly beaten
- ✓ ½ C. frozen green peas, thawed
- ✓ ½ C. frozen carrot, thawed
- ✓ 1 tsp. soy sauce
- ✓ 1 tsp. Sriracha sauce
- ✓ ½ tsp. sesame seeds, toasted

1. Grease a baking dish with cooking spray. Set aside.
2. In a large-sized bowl, add rice, vegetable oil, one tsp. of sesame oil, water, salt, and white pepper and mix well.
3. Place the rice mixture into the prepared baking dish.
4. Select "AIRFRY/SUPER CONVECTION" of Breville Smart Oven Air Fryer Pro and then adjust the temperature to 380 °F.
5. Adjust the time for 18 minutes and press "Start/Stop" to begin preheating.
6. As the unit beeps to show that it is preheated, arrange the baking dish over the wire rack.
7. Stir the rice mixture once halfway through.
8. After 12 minutes of cooking, place the beaten egg over rice.
9. After 15 minutes of cooking, stir in the peas and carrots.
10. Meanwhile, in a bowl, blend together soy sauce, Sriracha sauce, sesame seeds and the remaining sesame oil.
11. After cooking time is finished, remove the baking dish from oven and transfer the rice mixture into a serving bowl.
12. Drizzle with the sauce and serve.

Per Serving:
Calories: 438 | Fat: 8.6g | Carbs: 78g | Fiber: 2.7g | Protein: 9.5g

RICE & BEANS STEW
Prep Time: 15 mins. | Cook Time: 3½ hrs. | Serves: 6

- ✓ 3 (14 -oz.) cans vegetable broth
- ✓ 1 (15-oz.) can tomato puree
- ✓ 1 (15-oz.) can white beans, rinsed and drained
- ✓ ½ C. converted white rice
- ✓ ½ C. onion, chopped finely
- ✓ 2 garlic cloves, minced
- ✓ 1 tsp. dried basil, crushed
- ✓ Salt and freshly ground black pepper, as required
- ✓ 8 C. fresh spinach, chopped
- ✓ ¼ C. Parmesan cheese, shredded

1. In a Dutch oven that will fit in the Breville Smart Air Fryer Oven, place all the ingredients except for spinach and cheese and stir to combine.
2. Cover the pan with a lid.
3. Arrange the Dutch oven over the wire rack.
4. Press "Slow Cooker" of Breville Smart Air Fryer Oven and set on "High".
5. Adjust the timer of oven for 3½ hours and press "Start/Stop" to begin cooking.
6. In the last 15 minutes of cooking, stir in the spinach.
7. After cooking time is finished, remove the Dutch oven from oven.
8. Remove the lid of pan and serve hot with the topping of Parmesan cheese.

Per Serving:
Calories: 379 | Fat: 3.1g | Carbs: 64.9g | Fiber: 13.4g | Protein: 25.4g

MAC N' CHEESE
Prep Time: 10 mins. | Cook Time: 25 mins. | Serves: 6

- ✓ 2 C. cheddar cheese, shredded and divided
- ✓ 1 tsp. cornstarch
- ✓ 2 C. heavy whipping cream
- ✓ 2 C. dry macaroni

1. In a bowl, place 1½ C. of cheese and cornstarch and mix well. Set aside.
2. In a separate bowl, place the remaining cheese, whipping cream and macaroni and mix well.
3. Transfer the macaroni mixture into a baking dish that will fit in the Vortex Plus Air Fryer Oven.
4. With a piece of foil, cover the baking dish.
5. Select "AIRFRY/SUPER CONVECTION" of Breville Smart Oven Air Fryer Pro and then adjust the temperature to 310 °F.
6. Adjust the time for 25 minutes and press "Start/Stop" to begin preheating.
7. As the unit beeps to show that it is preheated, arrange the baking dish over the wire rack.
8. After 15 minutes, remove the foil and top the macaroni mixture with cornstarch mixture.
9. After cooking time is finished, remove the baking dish from oven and set aside to cool slightly.
10. Serve warm.

Per Serving:
Calories: 395 | Fat: 27.7g | Carbs: 22.9g | Fiber: 0.9g | Protein: 13.9g

SNACKS RECIPES

BUTTERED CASHEWS

Prep Time: 5 mins.| Cook Time: 5 mins.| Serves: 6

- ✓ 1½ C. raw cashews
- ✓ 1 tsp. unsalted butter, melted
- ✓ Salt and ground black pepper, as required

1. In a large-sized bowl, blend together all the ingredients.
2. Arrange the cashews into the air fryer basket.
3. Select "AIRFRY/SUPER CONVECTION" of Breville Smart Oven Air Fryer Pro and then adjust the temperature to 355 °F.
4. Adjust the time for 5 minutes and press "Start/Stop" to begin preheating.
5. As the unit beeps to show that it is preheated, insert the air fryer basket in the oven.
6. Shake the cashews once halfway through.
7. After cooking time is finished, remove the air fryer basket from oven and set aside to cool completely before serving.

Per Serving:
Calories: 202| Fat: 16.5g| Carbs: 11.2g| Fiber: 1g| Protein: 5.3g

APPLE CHIPS

Prep Time: 10 mins.| Cook Time: 8 mins.| Serves: 2

- ✓ 1 apple, peeled, cored and thinly sliced
- ✓ 1 tbsp. white sugar
- ✓ ½ tsp. ground cinnamon
- ✓ Pinch of ground cardamom
- ✓ Pinch of ground ginger
- ✓ Pinch of salt

1. In a large-sized bowl, add all ingredients and toss to coat well.
2. Arrange the apple chips into the air fryer basket.
3. Select "AIRFRY/SUPER CONVECTION" of Breville Smart Oven Air Fryer Pro and then adjust the temperature to 390 °F.
4. Adjust the time for 8 minutes and press "Start/Stop" to begin preheating.
5. As the unit beeps to show that it is preheated, insert the air fryer basket in the oven.
6. After cooking time is finished, remove the air fryer basket from oven and set aside to cool completely before serving.

Per Serving:
Calories: 83| Fat: 0.2g| Carbs: 22g| Fiber: 3.1g| Protein: 0.3g

TORTILLA CHIPS

Prep Time: 10 mins.| Cook Time: 3 mins.| Serves: 3

- ✓ 4 corn tortillas, cut into triangles
- ✓ 1 tbsp. olive oil
- ✓ Salt, as required

1. Coat each tortilla triangle with oil and then sprinkle each side with salt.
2. Arrange the tortilla chips into the air fryer basket.
3. Select "AIRFRY/SUPER CONVECTION" of Breville Smart Oven Air Fryer Pro and then adjust the temperature to 390 °F.
4. Adjust the time for 3 minutes and press "Start/Stop" to begin preheating.
5. As the unit beeps to show that it is preheated, insert the air fryer basket in the oven.
6. After cooking time is finished, remove the air fryer basket from oven and set aside to cool slightly before serving.
7. Serve warm.

Per Serving:
Calories: 110| Fat: 5.6g| Carbs: 14.3g| Fiber: 2g| Protein: 1.8g

FRENCH FRIES

Prep Time: 15 mins.| Cook Time: 30 mins.| Serves: 4

- ✓ 1 lb. potatoes, peeled and cut into strips
- ✓ 3 tbsp. olive oil
- ✓ ½ tsp. onion powder
- ✓ ½ tsp. garlic powder
- ✓ 1 tsp. paprika

1. In a large-sized bowl of water, soak the potato strips for about 1 hour.
2. Drain the potato strips well and pat them dry with paper towels.
3. In a large-sized bowl, add potato strips and the remaining ingredients and toss to coat well.
4. Arrange the potato fries into the air fryer basket.
5. Select "AIRFRY/SUPER CONVECTION" of Breville Smart Oven Air Fryer Pro and then adjust the temperature to 375 °F.
6. Adjust the time for 30 minutes and press "Start/Stop" to begin preheating.
7. As the unit beeps to show that it is preheated, insert the air fryer basket in the oven.
8. After cooking time is finished, remove the air fryer basket from oven and set aside to cool slightly before serving.
9. Serve warm.

Per Serving:
Calories: 172| Fat: 10.7g| Carbs: 18.6g| Fiber: 3g| Protein: 2.1g

BROCCOLI POPPERS

Prep Time: 15 mins.| Cook Time: 10 mins.| Serves: 6

- ✓ 2 tbsp. plain yogurt
- ✓ ½ tsp. red chili powder
- ✓ ¼ tsp. ground cumin
- ✓ ¼ tsp. ground turmeric
- ✓ Salt, as required
- ✓ 1 lb. broccoli, cut into small florets
- ✓ 2 tbsp. chickpea flour

1. In a bowl, blend together the yogurt and spices

2. Add broccoli and coat with marinade generously.
3. Refrigerate for about 20 minutes.
4. Arrange the broccoli florets into the air fryer basket.
5. Select "AIRFRY/SUPER CONVECTION" of Breville Smart Oven Air Fryer Pro and then adjust the temperature to 400 °F.
6. Adjust the time for 10 minutes and press "Start/Stop" to begin preheating.
7. As the unit beeps to show that it is preheated, insert the air fryer basket in the oven
8. After cooking time is finished, remove the air fryer basket from oven and set aside to cool slightly before serving.
9. Serve warm.

Per Serving:
Calories: 84| Fat: 5.1g| Carbs: 7.6g| Fiber: 3.1g| Protein: 4.5g

BACON CROQUETTES
Prep Time: 10 mins.| Cook Time: 5 mins.| Serves: 6

- ✓ 1 lb. sharp cheddar cheese block
- ✓ 1 lb. thin bacon slices
- ✓ 1 C. all-purpose flour
- ✓ 3 eggs
- ✓ 1 C. breadcrumbs
- ✓ Salt, as required
- ✓ ¼ C. olive oil

1. Cut the cheese block into 1-inch rectangular pieces.
2. Wrap 2 bacon slices around 1 piece of cheddar cheese, covering completely.
3. Repeat with the remaining bacon and cheese pieces.
4. Arrange the croquettes in a baking dish and freeze for about 5 minutes.
5. In a shallow dish, place the flour.
6. In a second dish, crack the eggs and whisk well.

7. In a third dish, blend together the breadcrumbs, salt, and oil.
8. Coat the croquettes with flour, then dip into beaten eggs and finally, coat with the breadcrumbs mixture.
9. Grease the air fryer basket of Breville Smart Oven Air Fryer Pro with cooking spray.
10. Arrange the croquettes into the prepared air fryer basket.
11. Select "AIRFRY/SUPER CONVECTION" of Breville Smart Oven Air Fryer Pro and then adjust the temperature to 390 °F.
12. Adjust the time for 8 minutes and press "Start/Stop" to begin preheating.
13. As the unit beeps to show that it is preheated, insert the air fryer basket in the oven.
14. After cooking time is finished, remove the air fryer basket from oven and set aside to cool slightly before serving.

Per Serving:
Calories: 964| Fat: 68.4g| Carbs: 31.1g| Fiber: 1.4g| Protein: 54.1g

BUFFALO CHICKEN WINGS
Prep Time: 15 mins.| Cook Time: 20 mins.| Serves: 4

- ✓ 2 lb. frozen chicken wings, drums and flats separated
- ✓ 2 tbsp. olive oil
- ✓ 2 tbsp. Buffalo sauce
- ✓ ½ tsp. red pepper flakes, crushed

✓ Salt, as required

1. Coat the chicken wings with oil evenly.
2. Arrange the chicken wings into the prepared air fryer basket.
3. Select "AIRFRY/SUPER CONVECTION" of Breville Smart Oven Air Fryer Pro and then adjust the temperature to 390 °F.
4. Adjust the time for 16 minutes and press "Start/Stop" to begin preheating.
5. As the unit beeps to show that it is preheated, insert the air fryer basket in the oven.
6. After 7 minutes, flip the wings.
7. Meanwhile, in a large-sized bowl, add buffalo sauce, red pepper flakes and salt and mix well.
8. After cooking time is finished, remove the air fryer basket from oven.
9. Transfer the wings into the bowl of Buffalo sauce and toss to coat well.
10. Serve immediately.

Per Serving:
Calories: 334| Fat: 13.8g| Carbs: 0.1g| Fiber: 0 g| Protein: 49.2g

FISH NUGGETS
Prep Time: 15 mins.| Cook Time: 8 mins.| Serves: 5

✓ Non-stick cooking spray
✓ 1 C. all-purpose flour
✓ 2 eggs
✓ ¾ C. seasoned breadcrumbs
✓ 2 tbsp. vegetable oil
✓ 1 lb. boneless haddock fillet, cut into strips

1. Grease the air fryer basket of Breville Smart Oven Air Fryer Pro with cooking spray.
2. In a shallow dish, place the flour.
3. In a second dish, crack the eggs and beat well.

4. In a third dish, mix together the breadcrumbs and oil.
5. Coat the nuggets with flour, then dip into beaten eggs and finally, coat with the breadcrumbs.
6. Arrange the nuggets into the prepared air fryer basket.
7. Select "AIRFRY/SUPER CONVECTION" of oven and then adjust the temperature to 390 °F.
8. Adjust the time for 8 minutes and press "Start/Stop" to begin preheating.
9. As the unit beeps to show that it is preheated, insert the air fryer basket in the oven.
10. After cooking time is finished, remove the air fryer basket from oven and set aside to cool slightly before serving.

Per Serving:
Calories: 311| Fat: 10.4g| Carbs: 29.4g| Fiber: 1.3g| Protein: 23.6g

MOZZARELLA STICKS
Prep Time: 15 mins.| Cook Time: 12 mins.| Serves: 3

✓ ¼ C. white flour
✓ 2 eggs
✓ 3 tbsp. whole milk
✓ 1 C. plain breadcrumbs
✓ 1 lb. mozzarella cheese block, cut into 3x½-inch sticks

1. In a shallow dish, place the flour.

2. In a second shallow dish, whisk together the eggs, and milk.
3. Place breadcrumbs in a third shallow dish.
4. Coat each mozzarella stick with flour, then dip into egg mixture and finally coat with the breadcrumbs
5. Arrange the mozzarella sticks into the air fryer basket.
6. Select "AIRFRY/SUPER CONVECTION" of Breville Smart Oven Air Fryer Pro and then adjust the temperature to 400 °F.
7. Adjust the time for 12 minutes and press "Start/Stop" to begin preheating
8. As the unit beeps to show that it is preheated, insert the air fryer basket in the oven.
9. After cooking time is finished, remove the air fryer basket from oven and set aside to cool slightly before serving.
10. Serve warm.

Per Serving:
Calories: 162 | Fat: 5.1g | Carbs: 20.1g | Fiber: 1g | Protein: 8.7g

CRISPY SHRIMP
Prep Time: 15 mins. | Cook Time: 8 mins. | Serves: 6

✓ 1 egg
✓ ½ lb. nacho chips, crushed
✓ 18 shrimp, peeled and deveined

1. In a shallow dish, beat the egg.
2. In another shallow dish, place the crushed nacho chips.
3. Coat the prawn into the egg and then roll into nacho chips.
4. Arrange the prawns into the prepared air fryer basket.
5. Select "AIRFRY/SUPER CONVECTION" of Breville Smart Oven Air Fryer Pro and then adjust the temperature to 355 °F.
6. Adjust the time for 8 minutes and press "Start/Stop" to begin preheating.

7. As the unit beeps to show that it is preheated, insert the air fryer basket in the oven.
8. After cooking time is finished, remove the air fryer basket from oven.
9. Serve immediately.

Per Serving:
Calories: 212 | Fat: 14.3g | Carbs: 1.3g | Fiber: 18.3g | Protein: 8.8g

PANCETTA-WRPPED PRAWNS
Prep Time: 10 mins. | Cook Time: 6 mins. | Serves: 6

✓ 1 lb. pancetta, thinly sliced
✓ 1 lb. prawns, peeled and deveined

1. Grease the air fryer basket of Breville Smart Oven Air Fryer Pro with cooking spray.
2. Wrap each prawn with one pancetta slice
3. Arrange the prawns into the baking pan and refrigerate for about 20 minutes.
4. Arrange the prawns into the prepared air fryer basket.
5. Select "AIRFRY/SUPER CONVECTION" of oven and then adjust the temperature to 390 °F.
6. Adjust the time for 6 minutes and press "Start/Stop" to begin preheating
7. As the unit beeps to show that it is preheated, insert the air fryer basket in the oven.
8. After cooking time is finished, remove the air fryer basket from oven.
9. Serve immediately.

Per Serving:
Calories: 499 | Fat: 32.9g | Carbs: 2.2g | Fiber: 0 g | Protein: 45.2g

FETA TATER TOTS
Prep Time: 15 mins. | Cook Time: 25 mins. | Serves: 6

- ✓ 2 lb. frozen tater tots
- ✓ ½ C. feta cheese, crumbled
- ✓ ½ C. tomato, chopped
- ✓ ¼ C. black olives, pitted and sliced
- ✓ ¼ C. red onion, chopped

1. Grease the air fryer basket of Breville Smart Oven Air Fryer Pro with cooking spray.
2. Arrange the tater tots into the prepared air fryer basket.
3. Select "AIRFRY/SUPER CONVECTION" of Breville Smart Oven Air Fryer Pro and then adjust the temperature to 450 °F.
4. Adjust the time for 15 minutes and press "Start/Stop" to begin preheating.
5. As the unit beeps to show that it is preheated, insert the air fryer basket in the oven.
6. After cooking time is finished, remove the air fryer basket from oven and transfer tots into a large-sized bowl.
7. Add feta cheese, tomatoes, olives and onion and toss to coat well.
8. Now, place the mixture into an enamel roasting pan.
9. Select "AIRFRY/SUPER CONVECTION" of Breville Smart Oven Air Fryer Pro and then adjust the temperature to 450 °F.
10. Adjust the time for 10 minutes and place the baking pan over the rack.
11. Select "Start/Stop" to begin cooking.
12. After cooking time is finished, remove the roasting pan from oven.
13. Serve warm.

Per Serving:
Calories: 322| Fat: 17.7g| Carbs: 37.9g| Fiber: 4.1g| Protein: 5.5g

CHEDDAR BISCUITS
Prep Time: 15 mins.| Cook Time: 10 mins.| Serves: 8

- ✓ 1/3 C. unbleached all-purpose flour
- ✓ 1/8 tsp. cayenne powder
- ✓ 1/8 tsp. smoked paprika
- ✓ Pinch of garlic powder
- ✓ Salt and ground black pepper, as required
- ✓ ½ C. sharp cheddar cheese, shredded
- ✓ 2 tbsp. unsalted butter, softened
- ✓ Non-stick cooking spray

1. Grease the air fryer basket of Breville Smart Oven Air Fryer Pro with cooking spray.
2. In a food processor, add flour, spices, salt and black pepper and pulse until well blended.
3. Add cheese and butter and pulse until a smooth dough forms.
4. Now place the dough onto a lightly floured surface.
5. Make 16 small equal-sized balls from the dough and press each slightly.
6. Arrange the biscuits into the prepared air fryer basket.
7. Select "BAKE" of oven and adjust the temperature to 330 °F.
8. Adjust the time for 10 minutes and press "Start/Stop" to begin preheating.
9. As the unit beeps to show that it is preheated, insert the air fryer basket in the oven.
10. After cooking time is finished, remove the air fryer basket from oven and place onto a wire rack for about 10 minutes.
11. Then invert the biscuits onto the wire rack to cool completely before serving.

Per Serving:
Calories: 73 | Fat: 5.3g | Carbs: 4.1g | Fiber: 0.2g | Protein: 2.3g

BEEF DIP

Prep Time: 15 mins. | Cook Time: 2 hrs. 5 mins. | Serves: 20

- ✓ 2 lb. lean ground beef
- ✓ 1 C. yellow onion, chopped
- ✓ 2 garlic cloves, minced
- ✓ 1 (4-oz.) can mild chile peppers, chopped
- ✓ 2 (6-oz.) cans tomato sauce
- ✓ 16 oz. cream cheese, cubed
- ✓ ½ C. Parmesan cheese, grated
- ✓ ½ C. ketchup
- ✓ 1 tsp. dried oregano
- ✓ 1½ tsp. red chili powder
- ✓ ½ tsp. ground cumin
- ✓ Salt and ground black pepper, as required

1. Heat a non-stick skillet over medium heat and cook the beef for about 4-5 minutes, stirring frequently.
2. Remove the skillet from heat and drain the grease.
3. Place the beef into a baking dish with remaining ingredients and stir to combine.
4. Spread the beef mixture in an even layer.
5. Arrange the baking dish over the wire rack.
6. Select "SLOW COOK" of Breville Smart Oven Air Fryer Pro and set on "Low".
7. Adjust the time for 2 hours and press "Start/Stop" to begin cooking.

8. After cooking time is finished, remove the baking dish from oven.
9. Serve hot.

Per Serving:
Calories: 188 | Fat: 11.5g | Carbs: 4.5g | Fiber: 0.9g | Protein: 16.8g

CHEESY ONION DIP

Prep Time: 10 mins. | Cook Time: 45 mins. | Serves: 10

- ✓ 2/3 C. onion, chopped
- ✓ 1 C. cheddar cheese, shredded
- ✓ ½ C. Swiss cheese, shredded
- ✓ ¼ C. Parmesan cheese, shredded
- ✓ 2/3 C. whipped Italian salad dressing
- ✓ ½ C. whole milk
- ✓ Salt, as required

1. In a large-sized bowl, add all ingredients and mix well.
2. Now place the dip mixture into a baking dish and spread in an even layer.
3. Select "BAKE" of Breville Smart Oven Air Fryer Pro and adjust the temperature to 375 °F.
4. Adjust the time for 45 minutes and press "Start/Stop" to begin preheating.
5. As the unit beeps to show that it is preheated, insert the baking dish in the oven.
6. After cooking time is finished, remove the baking dish from oven.
7. Serve hot.

Per Serving:
Calories: 117 | Fat: 9.4g | Carbs: 4.2g | Fiber: 0.2g | Protein: 4.4g

DESSERT RECIPES

SUGERED GRAPEFRUIT
Prep Time: 10 mins.| Cook Time: 10 mins.| Serves: 2

- ✓ 2 tbsp. white sugar
- ✓ 2 tsp. brown sugar
- ✓ 1 large grapefruit, halved
- ✓ Pinch of flaky sea salt

1. Grease the enamel roasting pan of Breville Smart Oven Air Fryer Pro with cooking spray. Set aside.
2. In a small-sized bowl, blend together both sugars.
3. Arrange the grapefruit halves onto the roasting pan, cut sides up and sprinkle with sugar mixture.
4. Select "BROIL" of oven and adjust the time for 5 minutes.
5. Select "Start/Stop" to begin preheating.
6. As the unit beeps to show that it is preheated, insert the roasting pan in the oven.
7. After cooking time is finished, remove the baking pan from oven and place the grapefruit halves onto serving plates.
8. Sprinkle with sea salt and serve.

Per Serving:
Calories: 77| Fat: 0.1g| Carbs: 20.1g| Fiber: 0.7g| Protein: 0.4g

GLAZED BANANA
Prep Time: 10 mins.| Cook Time: 10 mins.| Serves: 4

- ✓ 2 ripe bananas, peeled and sliced lengthwise
- ✓ 1 tsp. fresh lime juice
- ✓ 4 tsp. maple syrup
- ✓ 1/8 tsp. ground cinnamon

1. Arrange the banana halves onto the greased baking dish, cut sides up.
2. Drizzle the banana halves with maple syrup and sprinkle with cinnamon.
3. Select "AIRFRY/SUPER CONVECTION" of Breville Smart Oven Air Fryer Pro and then adjust the temperature to 350 °F.
4. Adjust the time for 10 minutes and press "Start/Stop" to begin preheating.
5. As the unit beeps to show that it is preheated, arrange the baking dish over the wire rack.
6. After cooking time is finished, remove the baking dish from oven.
7. Serve immediately.

Per Serving:
Calories: 74| Fat: 0.2g| Carbs: 19.4g| Fiber: 1.6g| Protein: 0.7g

GLAZED FIGS

Prep Time: 10 mins.| Cook Time: 10 mins.| Serves: 4

- ✓ 4 fresh figs
- ✓ 4 tsp. honey
- ✓ 2/3 C. Mascarpone cheese, softened
- ✓ Pinch of ground cinnamon

1. Line the enamel roasting pan of Breville Smart Oven Air Fryer Pro with parchment paper. Set aside.
2. Cut each fig into the quarter, leaving just a little at the base to hold the fruit together.
3. Arrange the figs onto the roasting pan and drizzle with honey.
4. Place about 2 tsp. of Mascarpone cheese in the center of each fig and sprinkle with cinnamon
5. Arrange the figs into the enamel roasting pan.
6. Select "BROIL" of oven and adjust the time for 15 minutes and press "Start/Stop" to begin preheating.
7. As the unit beeps to show that it is preheated, insert the roasting pan in the oven.
8. After cooking time is finished, remove the roasting pan from oven and transfer the figs onto serving plates.
9. Serve warm.

Per Serving:
Calories: 141| Fat: 5.5g| Carbs: 19.2g| Fiber: 1.9g| Protein: 5.3g

MARSHMALLOW PASTRIS

Prep Time: 10 mins.| Cook Time: 5 mins.| Serves: 4

- ✓ 4 phyllo pastry sheets, thawed
- ✓ 2 oz. butter, melted
- ✓ ¼ C. chunky peanut butter
- ✓ 4 tsp. marshmallow fluff
- ✓ Pinch of salt

1. Brush 1 sheet of phyllo with butter.
2. Place the second sheet of phyllo on top of the first one and brush it with butter.
3. Repeat until all 4 sheets are used.
4. Cut the phyllo layers in 4 (3x12-inch) equal-sized strips.
5. Place 1 tbsp. of peanut butter on the underside of a strip of phyllo and top with 1 tsp. of marshmallow fluff.
6. Carefully fold the tip of the sheet over the filling to make a triangle.
7. Then fold repeatedly in a zigzag manner until the filling is fully covered.
8. Grease the air fryer basket of Breville Smart Oven Air Fryer Pro with cooking spray.
9. Arrange the pastries into the prepared air fryer basket and insert in the oven.
10. Select "AIRFRY/SUPER CONVECTION" of oven and then adjust the temperature to 360 °F.
11. Adjust the time for 15 minutes and press "Start/Stop" to begin preheating.
12. As the unit beeps to show that it is preheated, insert the air fryer basket in the oven.
13. After cooking time is finished, remove the air fryer basket from oven and set aside to cool slightly.
14. Sprinkle each pastry with a pinch of salt and serve warm.

Per Serving:
Calories: 248| Fat: 20.5g| Carbs: 12.7g| Fiber: 1.3g| Protein: 5.2g

LEMON MOUSSE

Prep Time: 10 mins.| Cook Time: 12 mins.| Serves: 2

✓ 4 oz. cream cheese, softened
✓ ½ C. heavy cream
✓ 2 tbsp. fresh lemon juice
✓ 4-6 drops liquid stevia
✓ 2 pinches salt

1. In a large-sized bowl, add all ingredients and mix until well blended.
2. Transfer the mixture into 2 ramekins.
3. Select "BAKE" of Breville Smart Oven Air Fryer Pro and adjust the temperature to 350 °F.
4. Adjust the time for 12 minutes and press "Start/Stop" to begin preheating.
5. As the unit beeps to show that it is preheated, arrange the ramekins over the wire rack.
6. After cooking time is finished, remove the ramekins from oven and place onto a cooling rack to cool.
7. Refrigerate the ramekins for about 3-4 hours before serving.

Per Serving:
Calories: 354| Fat: 30.9g| Carbs: 15.9g| Fiber: 0 g| Protein: 4.9g

BANANA MUG CAKE
Prep Time: 10 mins.| Cook Time: 30 mins.| Serves: 2

✓ ½ C. all-purpose flour
✓ ½ tsp. baking soda
✓ ¼ tsp. ground cinnamon
✓ 1/8 tsp. salt

✓ 1 C. banana, peeled and mashed
✓ 4 tbsp. white sugar
✓ 2tbsp. unsalted butter, melted
✓ 2 egg yolks
✓ ¼ tsp. vanilla extract

1. Lightly grease 2 ramekins with cooking spray. Set aside.
2. In a bowl, blend together the flour, baking soda, cinnamon and salt.
3. In a separate bowl, add mashed banana and sugar and whisk well.
4. Add butter, the egg yolk, and the vanilla and mix well.
5. Add flour mixture and mix until just blended.
6. Place the cake mixture into the prepared ramekins evenly
7. Select "AIRFRY/SUPER CONVECTION" of Breville Smart Oven Air Fryer Pro and then adjust the temperature to 350 °F.
8. Adjust the time for 30 minutes and press "Start/Stop" to begin preheating.
9. As the unit beeps to show that it is preheated, arrange the ramekins over the wire rack.
10. After cooking time is finished, remove the ramekins from oven and set aside to cool slightly before serving.

Per Serving:
Calories: 430| Fat: 16.6g| Carbs: 66g| Fiber: 2.9g| Protein: 6.9g

STRAWBERRY DANISH
Prep Time: 15 mins.| Cook Time: 25 mins.| Serves: 6

- ✓ 1 tube full-sheet crescent roll dough
- ✓ 4 oz. cream cheese, softened
- ✓ ¼ C. strawberry jam
- ✓ ½ C. fresh strawberries, hulled and chopped
- ✓ Non-stick cooking spray
- ✓ 1 C. confectioner's sugar
- ✓ 2-3 tbsp. heavy cream

1. Place the sheet of crescent roll dough onto a flat surface and unroll it.
2. In a microwave-safe bowl, add cream cheese and microwave for about 20-30 seconds.
3. Remove from microwave and stir until creamy and smooth.
4. Spread the cream cheese over the dough sheet, followed by the strawberry jam.
5. Now, place the strawberry pieces evenly across the top.
6. From the short side, roll the dough and pinch the seam to seal.
7. Arrange a parchment paper into the enamel roasting pan of Breville Smart Oven Air Fryer Pro and then grease it with cooking spray.
8. Carefully curve the rolled pastry into a horseshoe shape and arrange into the prepared baking pan.
9. Select "AIRFRY/SUPER CONVECTION" of oven and then adjust the temperature to 350 °F.
10. Adjust the time for 25 minutes and press "Start/Stop" to begin preheating.

11. As the unit beeps to show that it is preheated, place the insert the roasting pan in the oven..
12. Flip the rolls once halfway through and spray with the cooking spray.
13. After cooking time is finished, remove the baking pan from oven and place onto a cooling rack to cool.
14. Meanwhile, in a bowl, blend together the confectioner's sugar and cream.
15. Drizzle the cream mixture over cooled Danish and serve.

Per Serving:
Calories: 335 | Fat: 15.3g | Carbs: 45.3g | Fiber: 0.7g | Protein: 4.4g

VANILLA CHEESECAKE
Prep Time: 15 mins. | Cook Time: 14 mins. | Serves: 6

- ✓ 1 C. honey graham cracker crumbs
- ✓ 2 tbsp. unsalted butter, softened
- ✓ 1 lb. cream cheese, softened
- ✓ ½ C. white sugar
- ✓ 2 large eggs
- ✓ ½ tsp. vanilla extract

1. Line a round baking pan with parchment paper.
2. For crust: in a bowl, add graham cracker crumbs and butter.
3. Arrange the crust into the prepared baking pan and press to smooth.
4. Select "AIRFRY/SUPER CONVECTION" of Breville Smart

Oven Air Fryer Pro and then adjust the temperature to 350 °F.

5. Adjust the time for 4 minutes and press "Start/Stop" to begin preheating.
6. As the unit beeps to show that it is preheated, place the baking pan over the rack.
7. After cooking time is finished, remove the baking pan from oven and set aside to cool for about 10 minutes.
8. Meanwhile, in a bowl, add cream cheese and sugar and whisk until smooth.
9. Now, place the eggs one at a time and whisk until the mixture becomes creamy.
10. Add vanilla extract and mix well.
11. Place the cream cheese mixture evenly over the crust.
12. Select "AIRFRY/SUPER CONVECTION" of Breville Smart Oven Air Fryer Pro and then adjust the temperature to 350 °F.
13. Adjust the time for 10 minutes and press "Start/Stop" to begin preheating.
14. As the unit beeps to show that it is preheated, place the baking pan over the rack.
15. After cooking time is finished, remove the baking pan from oven and set aside to cool completely.
16. Refrigerate overnight before serving.

Per Serving:
Calories: 470 | Fat: 33.9g | Carbs: 34.9g | Fiber: 0.5g | Protein: 9.4g

RUM CAKE
Prep Time: 15 mins. | Cook Time: 25 mins. | Serves: 6

- ✓ ½ package yellow cake mix
- ✓ ½ (3.4-oz.) package Jell-O instant pudding
- ✓ 2 eggs
- ✓ ¼ C. vegetable oil
- ✓ ¼ C. water
- ✓ ¼ C. dark rum

1. In a bowl, add all ingredients and with an electric mixer, beat until well blended.
2. Arrange a parchment paper in the bottom of a greased 8-inch pan.
3. , arrange a foil piece around the cake pan.
4. Place the mixture into the prepared cake pan and with the back of a spoon, smooth the top surface.
5. Select "AIRFRY/SUPER CONVECTION" of Breville Smart Oven Air Fryer Pro and then adjust the temperature to 325 °F.
6. Adjust the time for 25 minutes and press "Start/Stop" to begin preheating.
7. As the unit beeps to show that it is preheated, arrange the cake pan over the wire rack.
8. After cooking time is finished, remove the cake pan from oven and place onto a cooling rack to cool for at least 8-10 minutes.
9. Carefully remove the cake from cake pan and place onto the cooling rack to cool completely before cutting.
10. Cut into desired-sized slices and serve.

Per Serving:
Calories: 315 | Fat: 14.9g | Carbs: 36.5g | Fiber: 0.4g | Protein: 3.5g

CHERRY CLAFOUTIS
Prep Time: 15 mins. | Cook Time: 25 mins. | Serves: 4

- ✓ 1½ C. fresh cherries, pitted
- ✓ 3 tbsp. vodka
- ✓ ¼ C. all-purpose flour
- ✓ 2 tbsp. white sugar
- ✓ Pinch of salt
- ✓ ½ C. sour cream
- ✓ 1 egg
- ✓ 1 tbsp. unsalted butter
- ✓ ¼ C. powdered sugar

1. In a bowl, blend together the cherries and vodka.
2. In another large-sized bowl, blend together flour, sugar, and salt.
3. Add sour cream and egg and stir until a smooth dough forms.
4. Place flour mixture into a greased cake pan evenly.
5. Spread cherry mixture over the dough.
6. Then place butter on top in the form of dots.
7. Select "AIRFRY/SUPER CONVECTION" of Breville Smart Oven Air Fryer Pro and then adjust the temperature to 355 °F.
8. Adjust the time for 25 minutes and press "Start/Stop" to begin preheating.
9. As the unit beeps to show that it is preheated, arrange the cake pan over the wire rack.
10. After cooking time is finished, remove the cake pan from oven and place onto a cooling rack to cool for about 10-15 minutes before serving.
11. Carefully remove the Clafoutis from cake pan and place onto a platter.
12. Sprinkle the Clafoutis with powdered sugar.
13. Cut the Clafoutis into desired-sized slices and serve warm.

Per Serving:
Calories: 241 | Fat: 10.1g | Carbs: 27.1g | Fiber: 29g | Protein: 3.9g

SHOPPING LIST

Poultry, Meat & Seafood

cooked chicken
whole chicken
chicken legs
chicken drumsticks
chicken breasts
chicken thighs
whole turkey
turkey breast
turkey legs
ground turkey
cooked turkey
filet mignon
beef top roast
beef round roast
beef stew meat
beef shanks
ground beef
lamb shoulder
leg of lamb
rack of lamb
lamb loin chops
ground lamb
pork tenderloin
pork loin
pork chops
ground pork
ground sausage
bacon
pancetta
ham
salmon
smoked salmon
cod
tilapia
halibut
sea bass
haddock
shrimp
prawns
scallops
crabmeat
mussels

Dairy:

eggs
unsalted butter
whole milk
2% milk
yogurt
heavy whipping cream
heavy cream
sour cream
light cream
Mascarpone cheese
cream cheese
mozzarella cheese
Swiss cheese
Parmesan cheese
Parmigiano-Reggiano cheese
cheddar cheese
Monterrey Jack cheese
goat cheese
ricotta cheese

Vegetables & Fresh Herbs:

kale
spinach
arugula
zucchini
beet
potato
bell pepper
cauliflower
pumpkin
butternut squash
mushrooms
broccoli
green peas
carrot
celery
tomato
olives
onion
capers

scallion
garlic
ginger
jalapeño pepper
Serrano pepper
chile peppers
lemongrass
lemon
lime
basil
parsley
cilantro
oregano
thyme
rosemary
mint
dill
chives

Fruit

strawberries
cherries
banana
apple
orange
grapefruit
figs
avocado

Grains, Nuts & Seeds

white rice
brown rice
lentils
red kidney beans
black beans
white beans
oats
quinoa
pearl barley
wheat germ
macaroni
pecans
hazelnuts
walnuts
almonds
cashews

pumpkin seeds
sunflower seeds
flaxseeds
sesame seeds

Seasoning & Dried Herbs

salt
black pepper
cayenne powder
paprika
red chili powder
red pepper flakes
onion powder
garlic powder
lemon pepper
cinnamon
ginger
nutmeg
turmeric
cumin
coriander
garlic salt
allspice
curry powder
barbecue seasoning rub
Italian seasoning
old bay seasoning
Chile lime seasoning
thyme
oregano
basil
rosemary

Extra:

almond milk
coconut milk
olive oil
vegetable oil
sesame oil
Non-stick cooking spray
all-purpose flour
white flour
arrowroot flour
chickpea flour
cornstarch
active dry yeast

baking powder
baking soda
breadcrumbs
graham cracker crumbs
cornflakes
white sugar
powdered sugar
confectioner's sugar
brown sugar
maple syrup
honey
agave nectar
stevia
peanut butter
marshmallow fluff
balsamic vinegar
rice vinegar
vanilla extract
liquid smoke
soy sauce
Worcestershire sauce
fish sauce
chili sauce
Sriracha sauce
tomato paste
tomato puree
ketchup
tomato sauce
alfredo sauce
marinara sauce

Buffalo sauce
Italian dressing
ranch-style dressing mix
mayonnaise
Dijon mustard
dry mustard
dried cherries
dried blueberries
dried cranberries
dried apricots
chicken broth
beef broth
vegetable broth
cooking wine
white wine
dark rum
vodka
pita bread
whole-wheat bread
corn tortillas
nacho chips
coconut water
puff pastry
crescent roll dough
pumpkin filling
tofu
tater tots
yellow cake mix
Jell-O instant pudding

28 DAYS MEAL PLAN

	Breakfast	Lunch	Dinner	Total Calories
Day 1	Oats & Nuts Granola Calories: 302	Seasoned Veggies Calories: 88	Braised Beef Shanks Calories: 471	871
Day 2	Spinach & Egg Tart Calories: 231	Turkey Burgers Calories: 305	Beans & Quinoa Chili Calories: 397	933
Day 3	Cranberry & Oats Muffins Calories: 187	Broccoli Soup Calories: 179	Turkey with Pumpkin Calories: 457	823
Day 4	Eggs with Turkey Calories: 201	Pork Meatloaf Calories: 239	Rice & Beans Stew Calories: 379	819
Day 5	Yogurt Bread Calories: 157	Pita Bread Pizza Calories: 262	Balsamic Beef Top Roast Calories: 305	724
Day 6	Pumpkin Porridge Calories: 96	Vegetarian Loaf Calories: 229	Herbed Whole Chicken Calories: 435	760
Day 7	Chicken & Zucchini Omelet Calories: 209	Pork Stuffed Bell Peppers Calories: 293	Rice & Beans Soup Calories: 379	881
Day 9	Ham & Cream Muffins Calories: 156	Tofu in Sweet & Sour Sauce Calories: 115	Seasoned Pork Loin Calories: 421	692
Day 10	Garlicky Cheese Toasts Calories: 274	Pork Meatloaf Calories: 239	Glazed Halibut Calories: 218	731
Day 11	Pumpkin Pancakes Calories: 109	Beans Burgers Calories: 118	Chicken Cordon Bleu Calories: 672	899
Day 12	Three Grains Porridge Calories: 188	Stuffed Tomatoes Calories: 206	Ranch Tilapia Calories: 267	661
Day 13	Apple & Zucchini Bread Calories: 157	Mac n' Cheese Calories: 395	Marinated Chicken Thighs Calories: 286	838
Day 14	Cloud Eggs Calories: 87	Shrimp Scampi Calories: 245	Lamb & Apricot Casserole Calories: 377	709
Day 15	Garlicky Cheese Toasts Calories: 274	Chicken Kabobs Calories: 344	Haddock with Bell Peppers Calories: 166	784
Day 16	Ham & Cream Muffins Calories: 156	Crab Cakes Calories: 124	Rice & Beans Stew Calories: 379	659
Day 17	Three Grains	Pork Stuffed Bell	Spicy Chicken	

	Porridge Calories: 188	Peppers Calories: 293	Legs Calories: 402	883
Day 18	Bacon & Kale Frittata Calories: 293	Potato Gratin Calories: 233	Herbed Leg of Lamb Calories: 267	793
Day 19	Spinach & Egg Tart Calories: 231	Pita Bread Pizza Calories: 262	Crusted Salmon Calories: 446	939
Day 20	Yogurt Bread Calories: 157	Tofu with Broccoli Calories: 119	Bacon-Wrapped Filet Mignon Calories: 464	721
Day 21	Cloud Eggs Calories: 87	Scallops with Capers Sauce Calories: 224	Turkey & Beans Chili Calories: 457	768
Day 22	Pumpkin Porridge Calories: 96	Stuffed Zucchini Calories: 181	Beef & Tomato Curry Calories: 526	803
Day 23	Cranberry & Oats Muffins Calories: 187	Broccoli Soup Calories: 179	Crumbed Rack of Lamb Calories: 429	795
Day 24	Chicken & Zucchini Omelet Calories: 209	Vegetarian Loaf Calories: 229	Buttered Turkey Breast Calories: 333	771
Day 25	Pumpkin Pancakes Calories: 109	Chicken Kabobs Calories: 344	Salmon & Shrimp Stew Calories: 272	725
Day 26	Oats & Nuts Granola Calories: 302	Herbed Lamb Meatballs Calories: 285	Beans & Quinoa Chili Calories: 397	984
Day 27	Cloud Eggs Calories: 87	Vegetarian Loaf Calories: 229	Rosemary Turkey Legs Calories: 411	727
Day 28	Eggs with Turkey Calories: 201	Stuffed Zucchini Calories: 181	Pork with Mushrooms Calories: 276	658

CONCLUSION

The Breville Smart Oven Air Fryer Pro is a versatile appliance that can help you to cook healthy meals quickly and easily. It features a built-in air fryer, which circulates hot air around food to cook it evenly and crisp up the outside. The appliance also includes a dehydrate function, which can be used to make healthy snacks like dehydrated fruit or veggie chips. In addition, the Breville Smart Oven Air Fryer Pro has a slow cook function, which is perfect for making hearty stews and casseroles. With its multiple functions and user-friendly controls, the Breville Smart Oven Air Fryer Pro is an excellent choice for anyone who wants to eat healthier without sacrificing convenience.

INDEX

Made in the USA
Las Vegas, NV
09 November 2023

8051844OR00044